THE
MEMOIR
BOOK

'Patti Miller ... opens the poetic door to the brain, the door of memory and free association, where your writing is much more likely to be vivid and glowing with the intensity of the original lived experience.'

Susan Wyndham, *Sydney Morning Herald*

THE
MEMOIR
BOOK

PATTI MILLER

ALLEN&UNWIN

First published in 2007

Allen & Unwin
83 Alexander Street
Crows Nest NSW 2065
Australia
Phone: (61 2) 8425 0100
Fax: (61 2) 9906 2218
Email: info@allenandunwin.com
Web: www.allenandunwin.com

National Library of Australia
Cataloguing-in-Publication entry:

Miller, Patti, 1954– .
   The memoir book.

 ISBN 978 1 74114 906 7.

   1. Autobiography–Authorship. I. Title.

808.06692

Typeset in 11.5/13.5pt Bembo by Asset Typesetting Pty Ltd
Printed in Australia by McPherson's Printing Group

10 9 8 7 6 5 4 3 2 1

To Anthony

CONTENTS

PROLOGUE

How we — each one of us — live our lives, is still as fascinating to me as it has always been. Having worked with many hundreds of people on their life stories, the courage, humour, determination, passion and endless dazzling variety of individual lives continue to inspire and nourish my own life.

While *The Memoir Book* is an extension of my guide to autobiographical writing, *Writing Your Life: A Journey of Discovery*, it is also designed to be used independently. *The Memoir Book* focuses on memoir and the related genres of travel writing and the personal essay; it refreshes, develops and expands writing skills and issues introduced in *Writing Your Life*; and it explores concerns occurring further into the writing journey.

There are twelve chapters, arranged as a course, but you can dip in and use the writing exercises in any order you please. The chapters are based on live memoir-writing workshops and are informed by hundreds of manuscripts critiqued for other writers, as well as drawing on my own writing experience. Each chapter, except the first, includes writing exercises and extracts from published memoirs.

All writers, even the most experienced, at times need reminders of fundamental writing practices to help them head in the right direction. Or, perhaps, to find a new direction. I hope this book will do both. To me, the test of a useful writing book is whether you put it down and start writing — so I hope you will read *The Memoir Book*, the whole lot or a chapter, then put it down and pick up your pen or sit at your computer, ready to write.

1.
EXPLORING THE
TERRITORY

WHAT IS IT like for you to be here in the world? To me, that is one of the most interesting questions of all. It is the question I want to ask the tall Tahitian girl standing in the airport queue, the pallid man at the supermarket checkout, the grey-haired woman in the beribboned hat sitting on the beach, everyone I pass on the street.

What is it like for you to be in the world? What childhood dream, or perhaps dread, led you to this point in your life? What roads travelled, or less-travelled, have you taken? What do you believe about yourself? Do you feel most at home sitting by a fire in the country or dancing in a New York nightclub? Do you like rain on your face? How many sunrises have you seen? Do you have a compass and, if so, what is it made of?

What is it like for anyone to be in the world? This is the vast and private knowledge that each one of us has — and the great mystery. No one else can really know what it is like for you to be here on this planet. Others could conceivably know everything that has happened to you, your entire history, but they still could not know how you experience being here. For me, this is the starting point for auto-biographical writing and reading: a desire to express how one experiences the mystery and the journey of existing — its shape, its texture, its atmosphere — and a consuming curiosity to know how other people experience it.

Still, the desire to express one's experiences in writing is, by itself, not enough. Life is made of flesh and blood and tables and trees and office buildings; writing is made of words — can one level of reality be transmuted into the other? Post-modernist thought suggests that words can never repre-sent life; they can only represent a parallel world of words, a world of signs. Words are not a 'window' through which we can see reality, they are more like permanent contact lenses that construct the world we see according to the colour and thickness of the lens. More than that, the 'lens' also shapes our inner world. For example, our concept of the complex set of feelings and bodily responses we have in relation to another person is shaped by the words 'romantic love'. The feelings themselves are to some extent formed and shaped by the words. It is almost impossible to imagine (because we use words to imagine too) how we could experience the world without language. Still, acknowledging our 'lens', accepting that words will always form our perceptions and conceptions of our experience, we can still try to set down what and how we see through and with them.

The demand for autobiographical writing reveals that many of us share the desire to know what life is like for others. And many of us share the desire to tell our own stories. The journey of writing — in our case life writing, and more specifically 'memoir' — has its own paths and sign-posts and changing terrains to be explored.

Life writing? Autobiography? Memoir?

What *is* the difference between life writing and autobiography? Or autobiography and memoir? And what about 'memoirs' — add an 's' and is it something else again? Defining the territory could be useful before heading off on the journey.

There are many definitions, but let's agree that 'life writing' means non-fiction writing on subjects of personal experience and observation; it includes autobiography, biography, memoir, memoirs, personal essay, and travel and sojourn writing.

Autobiography is generally agreed to be an account of a whole life — from one's origins to the present. (For the most part *Writing Your Life: A Journey of Discovery* discussed how to write autobiography.) It can include some family history but concentrates on the individual life, exploring childhood experience, personal development, relationships, career — in fact anything that the autobiographer wants to include.

Biography seems clearly enough an account of someone else's life, although it too can spread out at its edges to include elements of memoir. The biographer can become part of the story. For example, *Poppy* by Drusilla Modjeska started out being a biography of her mother but became as much a memoir and even, in places, fiction.

Memoir is an aspect of a life shaped by any number of parameters, including time, place, topic or theme. One can write a memoir of childhood, or of a year in Turkmenistan, or of a relationship with a parent. While autobiography 'moves in a dutiful line from birth to fame, omitting nothing significant, memoir assumes the life and ignores most of it' (*Inventing the Truth,* William Zinsser). A memoir can be article length or book length. Travel and sojourn writing are also part of memoir, although they have some particular requirements of their own.

The distinctions become even more complicated when we consider memoirs, which naturally enough can easily be confused with memoir. Both memoir and memoirs are about an aspect of life, true, but memoirs have come to mean the reminiscences of the famous in relation to their public achievements. An army general or a politician might be expected to write memoirs — and in them we would expect insight into military campaigns or political machinations, rather than insight into the writer's relationship with their mother or other aspects of their private personality.

The personal essay is a genre closely related to memoir in that it often includes the writer's personal memories, but it is quite distinct in that memories are not included for their own sake, but at the service of an idea. Personal essays explore ideas and use a variety of elements — facts, imagination, humour and memories — to enhance that exploration.

While the focus of this book is memoir, there are many issues that apply just as much to general autobiographical writing. In most ways, the same concerns affect memoir and autobiography writers — and for you, the writer, the definitions and distinctions may not be relevant until your manuscript reaches the publisher, who must then decide how to categorise it!

Apart from categories, a memoir is simply an impression of being, a record of memory. Not long ago, I saw cave paintings in the Les Eyzies district in the south-west of France where Cro-Magnon tribesmen had painted images of bison, horses and ibex on the dark walls of their subterranean gallery. They had taken red iron oxide and black magnesium oxide and mixed them with clay and water and blown the mixture through bone pipes to create the drawings. As I gazed at the image of one magnificent bison painted fourteen thousand years ago — sensitively sketched, accurately proportioned — it struck me that the tribesman had, in a way, left a memoir. He had given me a small aspect of his experience, his perception of a significant part of his daily life. More than that, he let me see him recalling, selecting, concentrating, creating — being human.

Perhaps, as anthropologists have suggested, his purpose was magical rather than artistic. Perhaps he was trying to capture the strength of the bison for himself, or induce the bison to be captured. In any case, he was trying to accurately convey what he saw and understood, to express what was in his mind. It seemed to me that if this young man — as I imagined the artist — in an animal skin fourteen thousand years ago, felt the need to create a physical image of his experience, to record his perceptions, then it must be a necessary human activity. A pen or computer is not so different to a bone pipe, a drawing not so different to words. It affirmed my belief that it is not an indulgence, but a requirement of the human spirit to try to communicate the curious nature of being.

A confession

I probably should, here at the beginning, confess the true extent of my passion to know what life is like for other people. It goes back many years and has become a defining characteristic.

When I was fifteen, Pope Paul VI came to Australia — to Randwick racecourse in Sydney, to be exact. My father, being devoutly religious, wanted to see him, but since we lived four hundred kilometres from Sydney, an overnight stay was necessary. We had very little money and there were five children still living at home at that point, so it seemed impossible. However, my aunt, who worked in a motel on the western edge of the city, arranged for us all to stay there at a reduced rate.

The next morning we gathered at a small fibro church with the local parishioners and boarded a chartered bus which took us across the vast suburbs of the city all the way to Randwick racecourse. I can still remember my excitement, the feeling that surely this was going to be wonderful, life-changing, as I climbed down from the bus. We hurried in, but hundreds of thousands of people had already arrived and our group was well back from the altar constructed in the middle of the racecourse. All I could see was a tiny figure in the distance and all I could hear was faint, heavily accented English, the actual words barely discernible as a choppy wind blew them away. Despite my eagerness, revelation did not come.

But on the drive back across the endless suburbs, something did happen that changed my life. Seeing all those houses, all those gardens and front windows and curtains, I was suddenly and inexplicably overcome with a hunger to know what all the lives lived behind those curtains were really like. It pained me, a real, if dull pain in my solar plexus, that I did not — and could not — know how each life was experienced. What it was really like, not just what it looked like. *How is it for you to be in the world?* That's what I wanted to ask every person in the suburbs as they watched the television news and wondered at all those people crammed in the racecourse to see a tiny Italian man. That's what I wanted to ask all the parishioners sitting in the bus with me.

That's still what I want to know. *How is it for you to be in the world?* I feel the hunger to know when I travel on a train, or sit in a café, or stand in a queue at the supermarket, or visit my mother in her retirement village. I feel it when I am attending any gathering of people I don't know. I want to go up to each person and ask him or her, what is it like for you to be here in this world with only a set of stories to guide you? How do you do it? How do I do it?

Writing a memoir is a way of exploring that question. It is a genre wide and deep enough to allow us to explore any of the questions murmuring or shouting under a life, flexible enough for us to be able to evoke both the beauty and the terror of being here. Memoir is a vessel that changes according to what is put in it, sometimes it is formal and elegant, sometimes laid-back and laconic. In writing a memoir, you are returning to the well of literature, the place where you are trying to make words say what it is like to be here in the mystery of existing at all.

2.
FOLLOW THE HEAT —
BEGINNING, AGAIN

ONE OF MY favourite cartoons is by Australian cartoonist Michael Leunig. It shows a distressed man with wide-open, exhausted eyes, sitting in a doctor's consulting room. He says, desperately, 'Doctor, I have a book inside me.' The doctor reassures him that most people have a book in them and that he can refer him to a publisher. The man cries out that he just wants to be rid of it — to have it surgically removed, or dissolved with herbs, or some sort of therapy …

I understand completely this man's distress — sometimes it would be easier if the urge to write could be treated as an illness. The urge keeps growing, won't go away, but still it is difficult to know how or where to 'cure' it. You may not even have decided whether what you want to write is fiction or non-fiction — a short story, novel, or memoir. And what exactly is it going to be about? What shall you start with? And do you have enough material for it to be a book? Even if you are an experienced writer, finding the right genre, clarifying the subject and knowing where to start can seem daunting. Perhaps you have already started and you have come to a full stop. Given that you feel you have a book inside you — and given that you are not going to have surgery or try herbal remedies — what are the steps to take?

Clarifying your subject

What can a memoir be about? The short answer is: anything and everything. Here is a quick selection of memoirs from my bookshelf: *Cecilia* by Cecilia Inglis explores the experience of leaving a convent after thirty years as a nun; *Holy Cow* by Sarah Macdonald recounts a humorous search for truth in India; *The Blue Jay's Dance* by Louise Erdrich is a meditation on nature written during the first year after her baby was born; *A Thousand Days in Venice* by Marlena de Blasi tells the story of love at first sight in Venice; *Toast* by Nigel Slater is a chef's childhood memories of food; and *That Oceanic Feeling* by Fiona Capp explores a mid-life return to surfing. There is really no limit to the possible contents of memoir.

Memoir can explore any experience of being human and can be shaped by any number of parameters or themes. It can be delineated by a time and place: *Out of Africa*, by Karen Blixen; a relationship: *Velocity*, by Mandy Sayer; an illness: *Forever Today*, by Deborah Wearing; social issues: *Once in a House on Fire*, by Andrea Ashworth; a journey: *Desert Places* by Robyn Davidson; or even an abstract idea: *The Last One Who Remembers*, my own first memoir. Whatever you have done, whatever has happened to you, whatever concerns you, is a fit subject for memoir. Write any list of things that have happened in your life and you will have created a list of topics.

Sometimes you may not have clarified your subject, or its parameters. Don't let that stop you writing — if you wait until everything is clear and organised in your mind, you may never get started. Even without a properly defined subject, you can still start writing various memories and ideas that interest you. Your precise subject can emerge over time. The manuscript that became my second memoir, *Whatever The Gods Do*, began as notes on singing lessons I took one summer. Over a long period of time and many drafts, a memoir emerged about a friend who had died and my relationship to her young son. I had very little idea when I began what it would become, but the story itself seemed to know where it was going all along. It is important to learn to trust the gestation process that goes on underneath the conscious mind.

It doesn't mean that you can sit watching television and eating chocolate every evening and the story will grow perfectly formed inside you! But neither does it mean you should allow a lack of clear direction or shape to prevent you from starting. You can help the gestation process in a number of ways. For example, you can clarify your topic by doing some 'pre-writing' — that is, start writing the thoughts floating around in your head. You are not writing the memoir, you are writing about it. This 'pre-writing' is a ramble, a kind of scaffolding, from which you explore the general territory. It can be very helpful in clarifying the material and the worth of your story.

'Composting' your material is also useful. Often, experience feels monolithic and can take time to break down into usable writing elements. Many times in writing classes, students tackle events which are too recent, and not only are they overwhelmed by the events emotionally, they also find their writing 'lumpy' and raw, much like the original materials of a compost heap. Time is partly the solution. Write immediate impressions certainly, straight after a birth or death or divorce or whatever you have experienced, but do not expect that this will necessarily be the final or truest word on the matter.

Experience needs to be filtered through the weathers of the self, remade by the processes of reflection, until it finds its richest form. You can help this process along by 'digging' over the memory, that is, writing about different aspects of it, testing out ways of approaching it, experimenting with starting in different places. I recently watched a documentary about the creation of 'Imagine', the song by John Lennon, and it was fascinating and reassuring to see such an accomplished artist try and then discard all sorts of possible arrangements until he came up with the song that is an anthem of hope even today. The process of creation is not a straight line but an experimental process with lots of trial and error. Feel free to make mistakes!

Many people also advise jotting down ideas as they come to you but, personally, I've found if I write something down, it is then out of my head and therefore not contributing to the general composting going on in there. It usually just stays in the notebook, not going anywhere. I find it better to have a session of jotting things down so that the thoughts are all on one page and thus can be re-read still in relationship to one another. That way, the composting process continues on the page. However, everyone's method is different, so if the 'jotting things down when they occur' method works for you, keep it up.

It's important in the beginning to 'follow the heat', as one of my writing teachers said many years ago. Rather than working out the sensible or logical place to start your writing, begin with the idea or event that you feel most passionate about. It is true that if you spend too much time trying to decide on the rational place to start, you can lose the impetus to begin at all. Commence with the event or person that excites your interest, arouses your emotion — positive or negative. It doesn't mean you cannot change things around later, but begin with the heat, and follow the heat.

In relation to finding your subject, consider its length. Is it a short memoir, publishable in a magazine or collection, or is it book length? It is a key issue, for the wrong decision can result in too much material compressed, or too little material padded out — both common problems in manuscripts I have worked on. Sometimes, a subject which you thought might be a book turns out to be much more effective as a 5000 word memoir. Conversely, a short piece can keep growing as you find there is more and more under the surface and it can end up being a book length manuscript. A useful way to see if you have enough material for a book length memoir is to brainstorm your idea — see the first writing exercise later in this chapter.

Novel or memoir?

Should your story be a novel or a memoir? It might seem an obvious decision as a memoir relates stories about actual people and events, and a novel recounts imaginary people and events. But it is necessary to consider the issue because so many people have asked me whether they should write their life story 'as a novel'. I always answer that one doesn't write anything 'as a novel' — either it is a novel or it is not!

What I mean by this shorthand response is that a novel and a memoir are two different genres with different starting points and different literary requirements. A memoir must begin with and answer to the requirements of truthful exploration of an actual life; a novel must begin with and answer to the requirements of its own narrative structure. I believe that writing one's life story 'as a novel' undermines the integrity of both genres.

To write a successful novel, one must be free of 'what really happened'; one must let the needs of the characters and of the story dictate what unfolds. If you are writing your story 'as a novel', then you are lacking that essential freedom. Such novels often look and feel like thinly disguised autobiography, meaning that the 'fictional' characters and 'fictional' world of the novel are unconvincing.

The fresh engaging energy of an authentic voice is also most often lost when 'a memoir as novel' is attempted. In fact, this is the most crucial loss because the writing often becomes flat without the vitality of this personal voice. Most people writing in the first person, narrating their own life, have a voice that is at ease, confident. The change to the third person, and to the idea that this is a 'novel', often results in stiffness and a strained or contrived air.

I would not say that writing one's own story as a novel never works, but I do suggest that it requires a certain amount of writing experience to make it work. The impulse to write your life is not a novelist's impulse. Obviously, novelists 'mine' their own lives to write novels, but if your impulse is to write about your own life then, most often, that is what you ought to do.

It is clear that many people want to write their story 'as a novel' because their story is controversial in some way. There are family or friends who could be offended and distressed, individuals and institutions that may sue. It may simply be that they want their story told but wish to protect their own privacy. These are all valid reasons for fictionalising one's story, but it is important to realise that one can also be recognised (and sued) when a story is written 'as a novel'.

Look honestly at your story and its possible repercussions, and if it is important enough for you to write, then commit yourself to the truth as clearly as you perceive it. If you believe you cannot write what really happened but still want to explore the issues, then put aside the actual people and events, and consider writing a novel based on the essential issues or themes, or using a central narrative element of your own experience.

Leaping the hurdles to begin

Knowing you have that book inside you, knowing its general shape and size, how do you to start the process of putting it on the page? Everyone has different ways of starting, but in every case it involves leaping over several hurdles:

- *Does anyone want to read about my mad mother/trip to India/life on an olive farm? Is it worth it?* To jump over this one you must ask yourself not 'Does anyone want to read it?', but 'Do I want to write it? Is it important to me that it is written?' Once you are sure it is necessary for you to write it, then the hurdle of whether other people will want to read it falls to the ground.

  On the other hand, practically speaking, it might be that there have been a number of other books written on the topic and perhaps readers have had enough of renovating houses in Italy or growing up in a zany, dysfunctional family. In that case you need to make sure that your perspective on it is fresh and original. If you want to write your Italian renovation memoir, then read recent publications on the same topic, perhaps look at your story again and see if there is something singular about yours that will make it a unique story.

- *Do I have the right to tell the world about my mad mother/my boyfriend's infidelity/my nasty neighbours?* This is the trickiest question of all and one on which many memoirs founder. The anxiety induced by whether you have a right to tell the story can stop you in your tracks. This issue will be discussed in more detail in chapter 8, but in order to leap over at least the beginning hurdle, you need to ask yourself, once again: 'How important is this story to me?' If it has been deeply significant in your life, then, as a starting point, you have the right to tell it as part of your story. You can also try the Scarlett O'Hara trick — worry about that tomorrow. Tell yourself that this is only a first draft — you can take the controversial topic out later if it will cause a problem. That way you can at least overcome the initial paralysis.

- *Where in this huge tangle of events do I start?* This question can delay beginning very effectively, especially when your memoir covers a number of years and/or very complicated events. It can sometimes be difficult to discern the actual origins of the story you want to tell. If this is the case, then try the patchwork quilter's method — just start making small pieces. Don't try to decide whether or not you are writing the beginning, simply start writing particular pieces, the incidents or memories that you keep thinking about. (Follow the heat!) This acts as a kind of warming-up process — you don't start running in the Olympic Games without having done a bit of training and you don't start writing a book without doing a few warm-up exercises. These short pieces can be 300 words or 3000 words. It doesn't matter. Doing short pieces will help you gain or restore confidence and you will have made a start without having to leap over the biggest hurdle at the beginning.

- *I want to start but I just keep putting it off — how can I overcome the 'one day I'll do it' syndrome?* This endless delaying tactic usually comes from fear of failing: if you don't start, then it is always a perfect idea, unmarked by messy struggle. 'One day I am going to write a book' is much easier to handle than actually starting and not succeeding. This is a particularly tricky hurdle and a cunning strategy is needed to overcome it. Instead of having a vague 'one day I'll start', or a terrifying 'today I will start', give yourself a precise date in the near future — say, two or three weeks away — to commence. Make sure it's a convenient date — not when you are at work or on Mother's Day — write it on your calendar or in your diary, and then just keep it in mind. Work out which days of the week and times you can continue with the work. Pick a writing exercise from this book well beforehand. When the day comes, sit down and do the writing exercise. At first, only allow yourself half an hour for writing. Be strict; not a moment more. The combined strategies of a deliberately delayed start and a very limited writing time tend to lessen the anxiety and increase the desire and focus. Keep to the timed routine but after a few weeks give yourself an hour. Once you are well established in the writing, allow yourself as much time as possible.

- *What if I have started, but can't continue — how do I begin again?* That feeling of having come to a full stop can be depressing. The writing just won't go anywhere and you feel either uninspired, which is usually caused by over-planning, or utterly in a muddle, which is mostly caused by an early flaw in the structure.

  If overplanning is the problem then you may need to throw the plan to the winds for a while and tack out in a different direction. Write something you had not thought of before. Try a topic which is off the beat or at a tangent to what you have been writing about. Try making a short list, for example, of 'things that I am never going to include in this story', then write a paragraph on each. It could open up a new window, let a fresh breeze into your manuscript. Sometimes all you need is to get other parts of your brain firing, other neural pathways functioning. Do something different. Take a class in Mongolian chanting, walk in the woods, ask someone from another culture about their childhood.

If a flaw in the structure is the problem, it is very probably because you have not been honest about what is important or about the real causes of events. That might sound accusing, but it is easy to avoid the real issues and it often results in paralysing confusion later on. The solution is not simple; it might mean dismantling what you have done and throwing out a lot of material, which is never an easy task. Take a break of a few weeks then write a paragraph or two clarifying what you were trying to do in the manuscript, then re-read it to see if you can spot where you left the rails. If you can't see the problem, it can be useful to show it to someone else. A detached observer can often spot the gaping fault-line on which you have been trying to build. There will be more on troubleshooting structural problems in chapter 6, 'Finding Form'.

You will have observed that my preferred methods for dealing with hurdles are side-stepping them, or staring them down. Rather than backing away and giving up, or trying to leap over them and crashing down, it can often be best to either saunter around them — or to question whether they are really very substantial anyway and walk right over them.

READING

Are You Somebody?

by Nuala O'Faolain

When I was in my early thirties, and entering a bad period of my life, I was living in London on my own, working as a television producer with the BBC. The man who had absorbed me for ten years, and who I had been going to marry, had finally left. I came home one day to the flat in Islington and there was a note on the table saying 'Back Tuesday.' I knew he wouldn't come back, and he didn't. I didn't really want him to. We were exhausted. But still, I didn't know what to do. I used to sit in my chair every night and read and drink a lot of cheap white wine. I'd say 'hello' to the fridge when its motor turned itself on. One New Year's Eve I wished the announcer on Radio Three 'a Happy New Year to you, too.' I was very depressed. I asked the doctor to send me to a psychiatrist.

The psychiatrist was in an office in a hospital. 'Well, now, let's get your name right to begin with,' he said cheerfully. 'What is your name?' 'My name is ... my name is ...' I could not say my name. I cried, as if from an ocean of tears, for the rest of the hour. My self was too sorrowful to speak. And I was in the wrong place, in England. My name was a burden to me.

Not that the psychiatrist saw it like that. I only went to him once more, but I did manage to get a bit out about my background and about the way I was living. Eventually he said something that lifted a corner of the fog of unconsciousness. 'You are going to great trouble,' he said, 'and flying in the face of the facts of your life, to recreate your mother's life.' Once he said this, I could see it was true. Mammy sat in her chair in a flat in Dublin and read

and drank. Before she sat in the chair she was in bed. She
might venture shakily down to the pub. Then she would
totter home, and sit in her chair. Then she went to bed.
She had had to work the treadmill of feeding and clothing
and cleaning child after child for decades. Now all but
one of the nine had gone. My father had moved him and
her and that last one to a flat, and she sat there. She had
the money he gave her (never enough to slake her
anxieties). She had nothing to do, and there was nothing
she wanted to do, except drink and read.

And there was I — half her age, not dependant on
anyone, not tired or trapped, with an interesting well-paid
job, with freedom and health and occasional good looks.
Yet I was loyally creating her wasteland around myself.

One of the stories of my life has been the working out
in it of her powerful and damaging example. In
everything. Nothing matters except passion, she indicated.
It was what mattered to her, and she more or less sustained
a myth of passionate happiness for the first ten years of her
marriage. She didn't value any other kind of relationship.
She wasn't interested in friendship. If she had thoughts or
ideas, she never mentioned them. She was more like a shy
animal on the outskirts of human settlement than a person
within it. She read all the time, not to feed reflection, but
as part of her utter determination to avoid reflection.

As the title suggests, Nuala O'Faolain's memoir is shaped
around the question of identity and its relationship to
parental influences. From the beginning, it is clear that she is
jumping in the deep end, into the heart of the matter. It is a
wonderful example of 'following the heat'. As she says in her
introduction, '…eventually, when I was presented with an
opportunity to speak about myself, I grasped at it. "I'm on

my own anyway," I thought. "What have I to lose?" But I
needed to speak, too. I needed to howl.' Like the howl of
many artists before her, like the yawp of Walt Whitman and
the scream of Edvard Munch, her howl resounded in many
other hearts.

WRITING EXERCISES

1. *Brainstorm circles*

This is a way of seeing how much material you have stored
away in your mind on a particular topic. Start by drawing a
circle and writing in it the subject you think you want to
write about. It can be a word or a phrase, for example,
'Seasons' or 'Iraq 2003' or 'Michael and Cancer' or 'Mountain
Climbing in Peru'. Then you write the first association that
comes to mind, then the association that comes to mind from
that one, and so on. You free-associate from the previous
word, not back to the central word or phrase. When you have
reached the edge of the paper or come to a stop, go back to
the central word and start another line of association. Do this
five to ten times — see the diagram opposite where I have
free-associated from the word 'seasons'. They are my personal
associations and so are very idiosyncratic. You will end up
with a spider's web of interconnecting associations around
your central idea or image. It will give you an indication of
how rich — or not — your idea is, and it will give you a list
of possible pieces to write. *(20 minutes)*

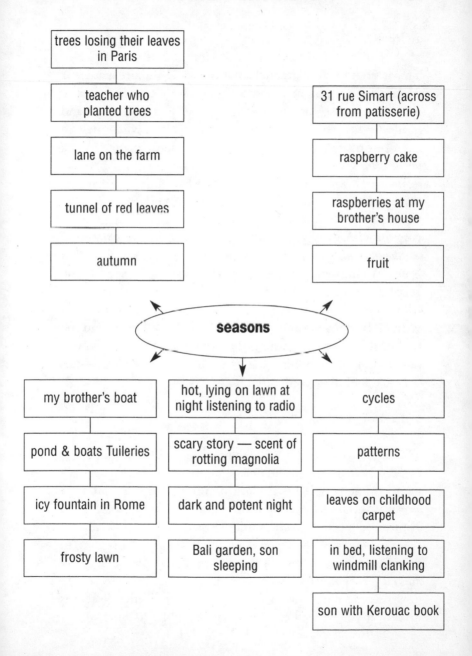

2. Ramble

This is useful if you are unclear about your subject matter or when you have, perhaps, just a vague idea. Start with a very uncertain phrase, that is, expressing how vague you feel, and head off with no clear direction in mind but a willingness to explore possibilities. For example, you might begin: *I feel I might want to explore that year I spent in London — I don't really know why. It's just that the image of that bare little room with the slatted bed keeps coming to mind. There was one picture on the wall, though, a poster of a mountain in Italy. Maybe that's why I went to Italy the following year. Perhaps that is what I want to write about — the little things which have changed my life ...* And then you keep on rambling! This exercise is meant to be very loose, very discursive — a way of loosening the order of the organising brain. Follow any train of thought that arises as you wander. It is not meant to yield good writing, but to find the trail. It is like sifting through the contents of a large drawer, not looking for anything in particular, but alert to treasures that may be uncovered. *(20 minutes)*

3. Locking editors in the closet

This is for writers who feel paralysed or blocked by a person or persons who might disapprove of the memoir. You simply name all the people who might be upset, disapproving or in any way limiting to your writing, and mentally lock them away in a cupboard in your mind — or send them to a tropical island if you wish — somewhere where they are not going to see what you are writing. Then start with the phrase, *It is very difficult for me to write about —* and continue. It is interesting how naming the problem you are having will often lessen its hold over you, at least enough to get started. *(20 minutes)*

4. Patchworking

This exercise is also useful for writers who know the general territory they want to write about, for example, 'Travelling Alone in South America', but do not have a clear idea of the story or thematic thread, or even if there is one. Write a short list of particular memories of the time — running into an old school friend in an Aztec ruin, getting lost in Buenos Aires, the sounds of the jungle — and start writing the pieces, one by one. Do not worry about the overall shape; simply make each piece as if you were making the pieces of a patchwork quilt. When you have written a few, then you can start looking at how they might be placed together, but to begin with, just concentrate on making the pieces. *(1 hour)*

5. Three beginnings

If you are clear on the subject of your memoir already, deliberately write three different beginnings from three different times in the story. Don't try to decide beforehand which one is the best place to start, just pick three intriguing places. Give each your full attention — as if this is 'the one'. After you have written them, see which one is the best. *(20 minutes on each)*

3.
THE IMPORTANCE OF MADELEINES — REMEMBERING

SHE [HIS MOTHER] sent out for one of those short, plump little cakes called 'petites madeleines,' which look as though they had been moulded in the fluted scallop of a pilgrim's shell. And soon, mechanically, weary after a dull day with the prospect of a depressing morrow, I raised to my lips a spoonful of tea in which I had soaked a morsel of the cake. No sooner had the warm liquid, and the crumbs with it, touched my palate than a shudder ran through my whole body, and I stopped, intent upon the extraordinary changes that were taking place. An exquisite pleasure had invaded my senses, but individual, detached, with no suggestions of its origin. And at once the vicissitudes of life had become indifferent to me, its disasters innocuous, its brevity illusory — this new sensation having had on me the effect which love has of filling me with a precious essence; or rather this essence was not in me, it was myself. Whence could it have come to me, this immortal joy? I was conscious that it was connected with the taste of tea and cake, but that it infinitely transcended these savors, could not, indeed, be of the same nature as theirs. Whence did it come from? What did it signify? How could I seize upon it and define it?

Marcel Proust

Ah, Marcel Proust's passage on the humble madeleines, one of the most famous in all of literature! But why? Doesn't it simply describe the taste of a little cake dunked in tea? Why is it so significant?

Well, it does begin a stream of memory which, a million or so words later, became one of literature's most intricate and significant works, Proust's *À la recherche du temps perdu* (*In Search of Lost Time*). A powerful little cake indeed. But for the purposes of the memoirist, it also contains a number of revelations about the nature and function of memory.

A sense of self is largely made up of memory. Without memory of events, relationships or knowledge, it would seem impossible to construct a sense of self and certainly impossible to write more than a few disjointed words. Understanding memory goes to the heart of who we are as human beings.

Memory is, always and everywhere, not just one of the memoir writer's subjects but also her means of working. Whether you are writing about your long ago childhood in a Yorkshire village, your career in Melbourne or New York, or the recent two years you struggled with your daughter's anorexia, you still need fresh and direct access to memory — not always as easy as it sounds. Often the mind will go blank when asked to remember a general period of life — for example, if I ask you to tell me about your schooldays, you will mostly likely say they were either good or bad — no detail springs immediately to mind. For direct access to memory, we need to look more closely at Proust's 'madeleines' passage. It reveals the significance of 'original' memory, its connection to the senses, its pleasure and pain, its central role in constructing a sense of self and, by implication, its crucial importance for writing.

Original and remembered memory

From observation and listening to others, it seems to me that we have two ways of experiencing memory: 'remembered' memory and 'original' memory. 'Remembered' memory is the most common experience; it's your daily recall of events of the immediate or faraway past which you either entertain in your mind or retell to others. This is the extracted idea of the memory; it is able to be sustained over time and can be quite clear, but there is a sense in which you are separate from the replayed memories. In fact, you feel you are 'watching' such memories, much as you watch a film. I can, for example, remember living in Paris for a year, the apartment I lived in, the streets I walked, the *boulangerie* on the corner diagonally opposite my building. As I recall these images, I am 'watching' a sustained and quite detailed memory.

'Original' memory comes more rarely and is, as Proust suggests, the product of a sensory stimulus of some kind. *Hot tea and cake.* A smell or taste or other sensory experience suddenly and powerfully brings the experience to mind. 'Original' memory is so strong and vivid that, for an instant, you relive the experience. *Standing in Aunt's bedroom eating cake.* This kind of memory cannot be sustained — Proust goes on to say that even retasting the madeleine and tea in the following moments does not give the same intense experience as the first taste. But it is very 'life-like', felt in the body as much as the mind — you are not so much 'watching' it, as immersed in it.

Just as significantly for the writer, 'original' memory can also be the first thread of a network of connected and detailed memories. For example, on a particular day last winter in Sydney, the combination of cold, rainy air and traffic smells suddenly created in me a distinct feeling of crossing the street in my old *quartier* in Paris. Not only did it feel as if the moment was happening again, but a series of memories rapidly unfolded of walking across the cobblestones towards the Pompidou Centre, of waiting in a café for my French teacher, and of the way I felt totally incapable of ever uttering a coherent French sentence!

Depending on the actual event being remembered, both kinds of memory can be intensely pleasurable, or painful, but in either case they create the sensation of being a continuous self, a sense of being a particular person. Both kinds of memory are necessary for the writer, but 'original' memory is especially important because of its 'life-likeness', because it is a 'close-up' of life rather than an overview or 'long shot', and because of its potential to unlock a whole series of memories providing both a rich flow and a connecting thread.

It might be helpful to look at how memory works, how it constructs your 'self', how it is triggered by sensory input, and how to use this knowledge to begin and continue your memoir.

Memory, science and writing

Reading memoirs and working with many writing students has led me to observe that all memories, whatever their nature, are stored with some kind of sense memory. Recent research on the nature of the mind and on memory has shown that there is indeed a strong link between the senses and memory. According to research using 'functional magnetic resonance imaging' (fMRI), whenever you have a sensory input, the amygdala — the part of the brain that determines the appropriate emotional response — 'lights up'. In other words, the connection between the senses and emotions is 'hard-wired' into the brain. As well, sensory memory appears to be spread across the brain, different sense memories being stored in different places — for example, the smell of the sea in one place, the sound of waves in another. What it means is that you only need one sensory aspect of the memory to be activated for all the rest to come flooding back. Some researchers call this the 'Proustian phenomenon'. It is the key to the memory-based approach to writing memoir rather than the topic-based approach.

Some texts on autobiography advise making lists of the various topics, with suggested lists of questions or topic headings such as 'parents', 'schooldays', 'holidays'. To me, this approach to writing is like colouring by numbers — you get the job done, but everyone's picture and story looks similar. Although the particular memories are different, they all have a similar flatness. This is because 'topics' are the result of logical organisation; they come from and are stored in the organising areas of the brain. If you start writing from a topic, then you are going into the rational, ordering network of the brain, which works by exclusion, by saying 'these things go in this list and not in that one'. It is a reasonable network, very useful for building bridges, organising an office and writing academic essays.

I believe it is important to write not from topics, but from individual memory. Memories are aroused and connect to one another not by orderly logical progression but, as we have seen, by a complex linking of senses and emotions across the brain. Memories connect via imagery, metaphor and metonymy — all poetic associations, which is why I believe *everyone's memory is a poet.* The smell of nutmeg might connect you not to other spices, as the logical side of the brain would have it, but to your father and the Golden Key café in a small country town where, for the first time, you tasted a malted milk with nutmeg sprinkled on top. (Experience and science both show that the sense of smell is the most powerful stimulus to memory. Research demonstrates that memories related to odours are both more emotional and more detailed.) Memory and creativity work in the same way, by inclusion, by saying 'all these things are infinitely connected!' If you start writing from a particular memory, it will give direct entry to the creative network of the brain. It is an associative network, very useful for painting a picture, solving a problem, or writing a memoir.

A quick refresher on metaphor and metonymy
Metaphor: a figure of speech where one thing is likened to another, for example, *my child grows in the cave within me,* where the womb is imagined as a cave.
Metonymy: a figure of speech where the part suggests the whole, for example, *the hand that rocks the cradle,* where 'hand' suggests the idea of 'mother'.

Writing via a particular memory will yield vividness of detail, originality, richness of flow, and even a structure.

'Original' memory is stored in such vivid detail that once you have the memory, all you need do is to write down the details. You don't have to 'think' of the lively details — they are there in the memory. It also means the details will be original and specific to you, to your individual experience of being, and not general memories of the times.

The network of associations between memories means that pulling out one memory and writing it down will inevitably pull out a whole connected chain of memories. Rather than being stuck on what to write next, you will find a rich flow, even an overwhelming flood, of memories demanding to be written!

Most intriguing of all, if you follow the seemingly chaotic patterns of memory, you will find a structure emerging. This is because of the poetic nature of memory connections — patterns form without your conscious direction. For further discussion of this idea, see chapter 6, 'Finding Form'.

Finding madeleines

The vital question is how to access both 'remembered' memory and 'original' memory whenever you need to. You cannot wait around hoping someone will offer you a madeleine. Besides, madeleines might not do a thing for you!

It is necessary to find your own 'madeleine' to have a way in to the labyrinth of memory. You can then begin to unlock some of the complex patterns stored inside.

Look to your sense memories first. Notice when a particular smell or sound arouses a sensation in you — follow the sensations that sweep through you and see where they lead. Notice all five senses — sight is often the only sense people think of using in their writing. Especially remember touch, the most intimate of all, but often the most neglected in memoir. The texture of skin, of cloth, of tree bark, of a car seat, is also part of the texture of experience.

Make lists of various precise sense memories. Look also to mementos you have kept — the name itself indicates their purpose. Take the time to listen to the details these emblems of memory may be able to tell you.

Everyone clearly has different 'madeleines', different keys which will unlock the flood of memory. Shirley Hazzard, author of the memoir *Greene on Capri*, speaking at a literary evening at the Village Voice bookshop in Paris, said that for her the key was light. She had a strong memory for different kinds of light in association with people and places and she only needed to see that light again for the memories to flow. Even as she spoke, her voice took on that quality which indicates a deep pleasure in memory, a pleasure Proust called 'reverie', a bright and dreamy experience which, he said, was his favourite emotional state and the one he believed all good writing ought to induce.

READING

The Diving Bell and the Butterfly
                              by Jean-Dominique Bauby

The Sausage

After every day's session on the vertical board, a stretcher-bearer wheels me from the rehabilitation room and parks me next to my bed, where I wait for the nurse's aides to swing me back between the sheets. And every day, since by now it is noon, the same stretcher-bearer wishes me a resolutely cheerful 'Bon appetit!', his way of saying 'See you tomorrow'. And of course, to wish me a hearty appetite is about the same as saying 'Merry Christmas' on 15 August or 'Goodnight' in broad daylight. In the last

eight months I have swallowed nothing save a few drops of
lemon-flavoured water and one half-teaspoon of yoghurt
which gurgled noisily down my windpipe. The feeding
test — as they grandly called this banquet — was not a
success. But no cause for alarm: I haven't starved. By means
of a tube threaded into my stomach, two or three bags of
brownish fluid provide my daily calorific needs. For
pleasure, I have to turn to the vivid memory of tastes and
smells, an inexhaustible reservoir of sensations. Once I was
a master of recycling leftovers. Now I cultivate the art of
simmering memories. You can sit down to table at any
hour, with no fuss or ceremony. If it's a restaurant, no need
to book. If I do the cooking, it is always a success. The
bourguignon is tender, the boeuf en gelée translucent, the
apricot pie possesses just the requisite tartness. Depending
on my mood, I treat myself to a dozen snails, a plate of
Alsatian sausage with sauerkraut, a bottle of late-vintage
golden Gewurztraminer, or else I savour a simple soft-
boiled egg with fingers of toast and lightly salted butter.
What a banquet! The yolk flows warmly over my palate
and down my throat. And indigestion is never a problem.
Naturally I use the finest ingredients: the freshest
vegetables, fish straight from the water, the most delicately
marbled meat. Everything must be done right. Just to
make sure, a friend sent me the recipe for authentic home-
made sausages, andouillettes de Troyes, with three different
kinds of meat braided in strips. Moreover, I scrupulously
observe the rhythm of the seasons. Just now I am cooling
my tastebuds with melon and red fruit. I leave oysters and
game for the autumn — should I feel like eating them, for
I am becoming careful, even ascetic in matters of diet. At
the outset of my protracted fast, deprivation sent me
constantly to my imaginary larder. I was gluttonous.

But today I could almost be content with a good old proletarian hard sausage trussed in netting and hanging permanently from the ceiling in some corner of my head. A knobbly Lyons rosette, for example, very dry and coarsely chopped. Every slice melts a little on your tongue before you start chewing it to extract all its flavour. The origin of my addiction to sausage goes back forty years. Although still at an age for sweets, I already preferred delicatessen meats, and my maternal grandfather's nurse noticed that whenever I visited the gloomy apartment on the Boulevard Raspail I would ask her in a beguiling lisp for a sausage. Skilled at indulging the desires of children and the elderly, she eventually pulled off a double coup, by giving me sausage and marrying my grandfather just before he died. My joy at receiving such a gift was in direct proportion to the annoyance these unexpected nuptials caused my family. I have only the vaguest picture of my grandfather: supine and stern-faced in the gloom, resembling Victor Hugo's portrait on the old five-hundred-franc notes in use at that time. I have a much clearer memory of the sausage lying incongruously among my Dinky toys and children's books.

I fear I will never eat a better sausage.

Bauby evokes a quintessentially French memory of the sensual delight of food. In the direst circumstances, deprived of movement and even the ability to eat, he creates for himself — and for us — the nourishment and pleasure of food. Read *The Diving Bell and the Butterfly* for its extraordinary awareness of the detail of life. It is perhaps worth knowing that, letter by letter, Bauby blinked this memoir (each blink like the jerky movement of a butterfly, hence the title) to his assistant after he was paralysed by a stroke.

WRITING EXERCISES

1. The senses

For each part of this exercise, when a particular memory comes up, start writing. Follow the memory wherever it goes, whatever it connects to. Keep writing until the associations run out.

Smell: Go to your kitchen cupboard, refrigerator, bathroom shelves, grocery shop, deli, garage, wherever, and collect together any jars, tubes, tins, containing anything from spices to sump oil, which relate to the time or place of your memoir. Put them on your desk, shut your eyes and then open the containers one by one and smell the contents. Select one that feels as if it has a strong association for you and concentrate on it. Don't try to remember, just concentrate on the smell. When a particular memory comes up, start writing.

Taste: Make a similar, but edible, collection. You might even cook some of the food from the time or place you are writing about. Notice the smells but also taste the food. When a particular memory comes up, start writing.

Sound: Find recordings of music. If it is music from your childhood or teenage years you may need to go to a speciality shop or search on the internet. If music was not part of your experience of the time, make a list of other sounds that were part of your experience and try to find those sounds — doors slamming, churchbells ringing, magpies carolling, brakes squealing. When a specific memory comes forward, start writing.

Touch: Make a collection of items to touch — silk, glass, sand, chenille. Touch your own skin — I find touching my cheekbones always brings back the memory of cupping my children's faces when they were babies. As before, when a specific memory comes forward, start writing.

Sight: The best sight stimulus is to visit actual sights, or to look at objects connected to the time and place you want to write about. If that is not possible, and often it is not, try to make a collection of photographs. When a specific memory comes forward, start writing.

2. Remembered senses

While the sensory experience is important, if it is difficult to gather the elements, or you don't have the time, you can write a list of sensory experiences — of smells, tastes, sounds, touches and sights. Of course, this way you are going in via the 'organising' side of your brain, but there are ways of finding a side door into the creative network of memory. The list must be very precise — don't write *the smell of roses,* but *the smell of the red rose just inside my grandmother's front gate*; not *the taste of popcorn* but *the taste of the warm popcorn I ate the first time I went to the cinema with a boy*; not *spices*, but *the bowls of cinnamon and cardamom in the souk in Marrakech*. Then select one of the sense memories and concentrate on it and see whether other connected sense memories come back. For example, the taste of popcorn at the cinema may bring back the feel of your legs on the leather seats, the sweaty palm of the boy holding your hand, the sound of the woman behind you rustling her packet of crisps. At any point, start writing, following the memory wherever it goes. Perhaps it will leap forward to other cinemas, other boys — it doesn't matter, simply follow it.

3. Hands

Call to mind hands you have noticed. They could be your grandmother's, your son's, your own hands. If you are not someone who especially notices hands, then use something else — eyes, smiles, gestures. Focus on one memory and try to evoke the whole complex set of associations these hands (or other physical feature) have for you. This is not an exercise in description — description for its own sake can be boring — but simply a way to find the sensory key to an emotional connection and thereby access the original memories.

4. Rooms

Take a pencil and paper and draw, in as much detail as you can, a room in which you have spent time. It can be a childhood bedroom, a backpacker dormitory in Barcelona, a university lecture hall, a doctor's waiting room, a bathroom in Paris, the kitchen at your father's house, a barn full of machinery — any kind of room. Drawing it will help bring back specific details, such as the feather pattern on the carpet in your childhood bedroom. Take only a few minutes, and then start writing. Again, this is not meant to be an exercise in description, but a way in to the creative network of memory. If it proves fruitful for you, it is an exercise you can keep using over and over to generate new material.

4.

THE STORYTELLER'S SEAT — NARRATING POSITION

ONCE UPON A *time, in a country far away* ... The ritual words are spoken and the storyteller has our attention. The centre of any story, fiction or non-fiction, fairytale or not, is the storyteller. The storyteller, or narrator, weaves the spell, en–chants (catches in a chant) the reader. As you spell out your story, the listeners and readers are caught and held by your voice. The voice of the storyteller is the sound connecting back to the beginning of human time; it is the voice spinning the strange shapes of words over what has happened, over both daily life and extraordinary events, pausing, rushing on, slowing down, throwing out a net to hold the moment.

The sound is heard in writing too, the sound of the storyteller on the page, the en–chanting voice when a story is being told. And when that story is about your own experiences, the storyteller is suddenly in a very confronting situation; you are required to be in two places, or two roles, at the same time, because you are both narrator and principal 'actor'. Which voice do you use, narrator or actor? How do you comment on yourself? Where do you stand — on stage or off? Do you leap back and forth between the two? Being narrator and central protagonist can obviously create a number of difficulties in relation to voice and narrative position.

Narrating position — voice

Voice conveys your attitude, your relationship to your life. Voice is more telling than anything you say — this is as true of writing as it is of the spoken word. A friend might say, 'I don't care about him anymore,' but you know from her voice that the opposite is true. In memoir, what you feel about your life, rather than what you think about it, will be revealed in the voice.

As the actor in your own life, you will have a wide variety of attitudes to yourself — perhaps ranging from disgust to admiration. As narrator, you will need to find and maintain a consistent attitude so that readers are able to align themselves with you. Readers gain their cues about how to relate to the material from the narrator. If, in conversation, someone keeps changing his attitude from anger to humour, from bitterness to gaiety, it is difficult for the listener to know how to react because the cues keep changing. The same is true for the reader. As narrator, it doesn't mean that you never vary your voice, but there does need to be a recognisable 'attitude' or relationship to the material, so that the reader knows how to relate to it, how to react. You, as narrator, must become the consistent observer of your own inconsistent life.

Listen to the voice in Sheridan Jobbins' 'Run Baby, Run', where she tells of her meeting with American Vice President Al Gore.

Scott and I decided, after a slow start to the morning, to head down to the Colorado River for a swim and a bit of considered hanging out. It didn't look like a lot happened down this way. Especially down here at Marble Canyon away from the action. We hadn't heard a car all morning, and the parking lot by the river was empty.

When we got into the water, it was surprisingly cold. I knew it came from snowmelt, but it was now late summer and I thought the water might have been warmer. Even so, the day was hot and it was perfect for a dip and a bake in the sun. I stripped to my Washington-bought, white, sporty underwear and stretched out on my clothes.

Scott and I were talking idly when we became aware of a shuffling in the underbrush. It was an unusual noise, which made me grab for my clothing. It didn't sound random like an animal. It sounded like a peeping Tom. Scott, in his machismo and shorts, went to investigate, and came back saying there were a lot of Tarago vans with blackened windows in the previously vacant parking bay. 'There are men in suits crawling on the ground under Betty [the car],' he said with an amused air of excitement. I stood up to get a better look and, sure enough, the place was crawling with people in suits and sunglasses. An emergency ambulance was on stand-by and a lot of men were talking into their collars and sleeves.

The noise in the bushes revealed itself to be another man in a suit. 'What are you doing?' I asked in an imperious voice, which I must return to my mother.

'Just a standard security check,' he said in a tone I presume he hoped was reassuring.

'That's pretty thorough,' I replied, making little allowance for the fact I was standing in front of him in my underwear, 'have you found anything insecure?'

He blushed. 'Have a nice day, ma'am,' he said and moved away.

Scott followed him. 'Is someone important coming?'

He didn't have time to reply when Al and Tipper appeared out of another blackened Tarago van along with some members of their family and a few other (presumably) CIA agents looking very stiff in their white-water rafting gear.

What an absolute shriek. I waved. There was a moment's hesitation, where the Vice President decided whether or not it was correct to wave at Double D Woman in her bra and panties — but then, lightly, raised his hand in a casual salute.

They all got on the raft and drifted down the river. We got in the car and drove to the Grand Canyon.

The humorous voice is unmistakable — the readers know where to align themselves, how to react. We are standing with the narrator, looking at her life with amusement. In this next extract by Jobbins, there is a slight shift in voice.

I haven't been on many dates, I'm not very good at them. My hands get sweaty and I don't know what to do with them. As a teenager on one of my rare dates I filled a sock with talcum powder and put it in my pocket. If my hands got sweaty I could squeeze the sock (that sounds like a euphemism, doesn't it?) and my hand would be made soft and dry.

Sorted.

My pimply beau had chosen the movies as the venue for our fumbly, nervous meeting. Sitting in the dark he made his move — slowly, you understand, very slowly. A sly hand passing over my shoulder. Stopping for a moment. A gentle stroking on my neck. And stopping. A small circling of my hair ... My hands got extremely sweaty with the encroaching excitement, but I was prepared, and squeezed my sock.

Eventually we got to pashing (necking, petting, parking, snogging) and were happy. It wasn't until we were blinking in the broad light of the foyer that I shyly looked at my brand new boyfriend and saw, to my enduring horror, that his black sloppy joe was covered (and I mean all over) with my white talcum-encrusted hand prints.

And that wasn't even my most embarrassing date.

Again, the voice is unmistakable, again the reader laughs, but this time there is a certain embarrassment in the laughter. The reader feels the narrator still squirming at the memory, and so the reader squirms too. That's fine — make your reader feel it. Jobbins has judged her relationship to the material — and to the reader — well. But sometimes, a narrator can be overwhelmed by her material and the voice can become distorted.

In one of my own memoirs, *Whatever The Gods Do*, I wrote several scenes about singing classes I had taken one summer. I was very unconfident about singing and, during the actual lessons, I felt overwhelmed by a sense of inadequacy. In early drafts, that sense of inadequacy swamped me as I wrote the scenes, so that the writing voice became unconfident. My dauntless editor pointed it out to me, saying that it was jarring and uncomfortable for the reader. She said it was as if I had

suddenly started playing 'Roll Out the Barrel' in the middle
of a Bach concerto. I had let the feelings in the material, the
feelings of the 'actor', overwhelm the 'narrator'. It was
necessary to step back from the material, step back to the
position of the narrator again to rewrite the story.

If you feel your material is overwhelming and distorting
your voice, consciously step back to the position of narrator.
In every case, the first step in finding your relationship to the
material is moving into the position of observer. This is an
inner process, a kind of detachment, which all writers
cultivate to varying degrees.

The narrating voice can also be affected by 'performance
anxiety', which happens when you feel very conscious of
your readers and their reactions. It can be a specific anxiety
regarding particular topics that you believe could upset your
family or friends, or a more general worry that the public
may criticise your writing. It can make your voice too
careful on the one hand, or too 'try hard', that is, straining for
literary effect, on the other. It can even stop you writing
altogether. All of these concerns about other people's
judgments need to be bundled together, tied up tightly and
locked in a drawer — at least while you write the first draft.
A first draft needs to be written freely, without worrying
what anyone else will think. There will be opportunities in
later drafts to address the possibly legitimate concerns of
other people. In the first instance you, as storyteller, must feel
free to tell your story in your own way.

Narrating position — distance

As narrator, you are in a relationship with your readers. They
are listening to you, sympathising with you, being charmed
by you, perhaps disagreeing with you. As in all relationships,

there is the issue of 'space', meaning how close or distant you are to your reader. Some people like to stand very close, to reveal intimate details on first meeting, to lay bare their emotions. Others are reserved, keeping their emotions to themselves or describing them from an analytical distance. The same kind of sense of 'personal space' operates in the writer–reader relationship and it is you, the writer, who determines how close or distant it will be. You decide how close you want your reader to be by deciding how close you will be to your material. *The distance at which the writer stands from her material is exactly the distance the reader will feel.*

Writing which is too close for too long can be disturbing for the reader, just as it can be disturbing if a person one doesn't know well stands too near during a conversation or reveals information which is too intimate for the relationship you have with them. On the other hand, a voice which is too distant can make your memoir feel cold and will not engage the reader.

Interestingly, a sense of closeness or distance is not a matter of *what* you reveal, but *how* you reveal it — where you, as narrator, stand in relation to the experience and whether, in fact, you write about it from *inside* or *outside*. Catherine Millet, in *The Sexual Life of Catherine M*, reveals very personal details about her sexual practices but with such detachment that the reader never feels pushed up too close to the experience. Millet is outside the experience as she writes, watching herself, thus putting the reader in the position of voyeur rather than participant. Perhaps you do not want your readers to feel voyeuristic either, and in that case there is always discretion! If, however, you want to write about very personal material, it could be useful to step back and write it from a more detached perspective.

If you want to draw the reader closer rather than keep

them back, write from inside your material, as though you are reliving the experience as you write it. It requires a leap into stored 'original' memory and, depending on the nature of the memory, can be emotionally painful. It does, however, give the reader a powerful up-close taste of the experience. Listen to Jenette McGrory in this extract from 'Train Crash'.

Where are we? The Glenbrook tunnel? Have we hit the side of it? There's a gorge near here. We are not safe! We could be about to fall. Does anybody know what has happened? How will they find out? When will they come? We've got to get out! I try to move out of my seat. I've got to get out. It's not safe and I must get away from the images of death so close to me. I can't get out of my seat. I'm going to vomit. I am so dizzy I fear I am going to collapse. Every time I try to stand up I am propelled back into my seat. I don't understand this. I am very confused and disorientated. I can't breathe properly. It feels like the air has been sucked out of the carriage and the atmosphere feels dense and thick with dust. I am afraid. I say to the woman next to me, 'I feel like I can't breathe, do you feel like that?'

'It's because the air conditioner isn't working.' I look around at everyone in the compartment. We're all going to suffocate. We'll all die here!

I am lost in a world of olive green, the colour of puke, and I feel just as unhinged as the seats all around me. Shafts of light enter the dimness, revealing the flecks of dust and grit that fill the air. The putrid musty odour chokes my air passages and leaves a faint metallic taste on my tongue. I can't breathe.

The reader is placed very close indeed, right inside the raw experience, just as McGrory was when she wrote it.

The narrator can draw further back, and hence let the reader step back, by writing from 'outside' the experience, as McGrory does later in her story.

> For several months after the train crash I felt as if I were two selves operating at the same time. One part of me was trying to function as normal and relate to the outside world. I would be participating in normal activities, such as having conversations with my colleagues, working on the computer or just eating my lunch. At the same time, my second self seemed to watch from outside, constantly vigilant to assess how safe things were and how well I was coping. This second self was also engaged in attempting to deal with the horrific images that were continually in the back of my mind, competing in a never-ending battle for my attention. The grotesque images were so real it was as if they had just happened, or were about to happen, so that my body reacted as if in a constant state of alert. Even when I gave in to their demands and allowed myself to focus on the memories, following them to their ghastly conclusion, they were not satisfied, demanding to be replayed over and over again.

Here McGrory has stepped back and taken control, writing from the intellect rather than from raw emotion.

Being aware of closeness and distance as a narrator means you can consciously choose how close to your material you want to be. It also means you can move closer or further away as you wish. If your material is too overwhelming, mentally stepping 'outside' it and then writing from that detached perspective may give you the control you require. If you see that your writing is becoming too dry, too cold, then you can take the plunge into the experience, remember the lived feel of it and write it as if you were reliving it. You could even try writing it in the present tense to give a vivid sense of immediacy and closeness.

Narrative distance is also influenced by whether one is writing from the point of view of a child or adult. Writing from a child's perspective will inevitably bring you as narrator, and thus the reader, closer to the material. Sometimes, if the child's perspective is too intense and unreflective, it can become claustrophobic for the reader. A shift to the adult perspective on the same material will result in a feeling of space.

The sense of 'space' is, naturally, a very individual experience. If you characteristically write 'close-up', some readers may criticise you for being too self-absorbed, while others will love the intimacy. If you write in a more detached way, some readers may find you too cool, but others will revel in the drier intellectual atmosphere. It is up to you as the narrator to find the distance that suits you and your material.

Narrating position — time of telling

In any story, but especially in autobiographical narrative, where the narrator and central protagonist are the same person, the 'time of telling' or 'time of narration' needs to be clearly established as you write, meaning that the narrator needs to be telling the story from a particular point in time. If the time the narrator is recounting from is unclear — and in particular, where the present tense is used for a number of different time frames — it can create confusion in the reader. The reader needs to know whether the narrator is describing events as they happen and is therefore unaware of how things turn out, or from a point in the future where she does know what happens. This might sound complicated and unnecessarily technical, but it is an issue that creates problems in many first drafts. Let me illustrate with an example.

Sally sent me a manuscript recounting her travels in Europe. She began her story at the age she is now, thirty years old, living in London, and then moved back in time to when she set out overseas from New Zealand with her boyfriend at the age of nineteen. So far it was clear that the narrator was writing from the present about her youthful adventures. But then the narrator began saying things that seemed very naïve for a thirty year old. It struck me that she was now writing from her younger self's perspective — in other words the 'time of telling' was now ten years earlier. I suspected that Sally had transcribed journals or emails written when she was nineteen (a suspicion that turned out to be correct). The effect was confusion — as if listening to someone who speaks like a child one moment and like an adult the next, making it difficult to know how to relate to them. The solution was simple: she needed to signal clearly which 'time of telling' was operating at any given point, using a device such as journal dates — *Ibiza 23rd April '91* — or presenting the material in email format when she was narrating from her nineteen year old self, and straight-forward text when she was writing from her thirty year old self.

If you want to tell a story from the point of view of both the time it happened in the past and from 'now', then you do need to signal in some way the shift from one narrating time to another. In some cases a layout device, such as a line space between narrators, can be enough to signal the shift in 'time of telling'.

The problem can be exacerbated if you use the present tense for both the time of telling and for events in the past. It can make it difficult for the reader to discern which 'present' you are referring to. For example, Malia wrote a memoir about her father, who left her mother when Malia was three years old. She used the present tense to explore her present (time of writing) feelings and attitudes: *I understand that my father is a flawed and limited man and I wonder if I can forgive him.* She also used the present tense to write about a period when she sought out and found her father when she was a young woman: *He is the man I have imagined all my life and I will never let him go.* Then the present tense for a later time when he again disappeared from her life: *I do not think he will ever understand what he has done to me. I can never forgive him.* Sometimes, depending on the context, it was clear which time period she was talking about, but often it was difficult to know whether she was writing about her present or her past feelings. In this case I suggested she retain the present tense for the time of writing, but use the past tense for all the past events.

If you do want to use a number of present tenses, perhaps for the freshness and immediacy the present tense can create, you will need to signal the different times — perhaps with dates, or place names, or a clear unambiguous context.

When you are interweaving a number of different times, the time of telling can become very complicated. In *Whatever The Gods Do*, the memoir about Dina, my friend who died, there were a number of different times I wanted to write about: the years of friendship when all was well, the intensive period when Dina was ill, the period when her son stayed with me every weekend after she died, the summer he left, the subsequent year when I visited him and he came back to visit me. To make it more complicated, I included the episode of my father's death, which occurred after these events, as well as incidents from my childhood many years earlier!

To manage all these time frames, it was necessary to have a very clearly indicated 'time of telling' from which I could easily move around the various sequences. I used a 'framing device', in this case a sojourn at a beach-house where I had spent several weeks sifting through the various elements of the story. What this meant in practice was that I referred to the beach-house a number of times in the narrative so that the reader knew I was narrating all these events from the perspective of a particular time several years afterwards. (See chapter 6, 'Finding Form' for further discussion of framing devices.)

To move about through the various times and not lose the reader, it was also necessary to regularly use 'directive' or 'locating' phrases. These are phrases like *It was a summer that makes me think now of paths crossing* ... or *I have come to this beach-house here on the coastal lagoon* ... or *It was about a month after the haemorrhage* or *I have The Book open in front of me now* or *One day when I was a teenager* ... All these phrases are at the beginning of paragraphs and immediately locate the reader in relation to the 'time of telling'. The narrator is always 'at the beach-house' and locates the various times in relation to each other and in relation to the 'present'.

A 'time of narrating' can be implied. It does not have to be constructed in the text as a particular time and place. Often it is clear that you are writing from 'now' and there is no confusion. As narrator, you hold all the story threads in your hands. Your perspective on the threads — where you stand in relation to your material — will have a key influence on the texture of your story. Trust your storyteller, claim and tell the story in your own distinctive voice, and draw your readers into the spell of your story.

READING

Swimming to Cambodia

by Spalding Gray

Now what I had to say in my scene with Sam was
simple — it was a little technical, but simple: 'A computer
malfunction put out the wrong set of co-ordinates. Seems
a single B-52 opened up over Neak Luong. There's a
homing beacon right in the middle of town. Check it
out, Sid.'

All right. Simple enough … for some actors. But *this*
actor needs images for technical words like that. I have to
build my own internal film, you see, or I can't remember
the words.

By the way, I played one of those American officials
who flew into Neak Luong. We were at an old garbage
dump that they had made into Neak Luong, right outside
Bangkok. The assistant director said, 'Would the artists
please get on the choppers.' Now there is no way I would
ordinarily get on a helicopter, but he called me an artist
and hop, hop, I was right on that chopper like Pavlov's
dog. They said it was only going to go up ten feet and
then just land. All they needed was a shot of the embassy
officials jumping off the choppers.

So I got on the helicopter and it went BRRRRRRR
— straight up. Straight up above this incredible jungle.
I felt like I was in a movie, like I was in *Apocalypse Now*,
and then I realized that I *was* in a movie! They were
filming me, and I had no fear, even though the door was
wide open and I was looking down. Craig T. Nelson
was practically falling out the door — we had no safety
belts — but I suddenly had no fear because the camera

eroticizes the space. It protects you like Colgate Guard-All.
Even if the chopper crashed, at least there would be the
rushes, right? My friends could show them on New Year's
Eve at the Performing Garage.

We went up six times and the feeling was triumphant.
I was looking up the Chao Phraya river and I saw, my
God, how much area the film controlled! Twenty square
miles of Thai jungle, all the way up the river, there were
Thai peasants throwing more rubber tyres on the fire to
make black smoke, to make it look like war, and I thought,
of course! WAR THERAPY. Every country should make
a major war movie every year. It would put a lot of people
to work, help them get their rocks off. And when you land
in that jungle, you don't have to Method-act. When those
helicopter blades are whirring overhead, you shout to be
heard. You don't have to Method-act when you look down
and see a Thai peasant covered with chicken giblets and
fake blood in 110-degree weather for fifteen hours a day
for five dollars a day. (If they're real amputees they get
seven-fifty.) It's just like the real event! ...

... 'Okay, boys and girls, let's go. Take sixty-four.'

It was a night shoot and we were up to take sixty-four.
And it was just the first scene of the night. I thought I had
it down. 'A computer malfunction put out the wrong set of
co-ordinates. It seems a single B-52 opened up over Neak
Luong. There's a ...' and I couldn't get the image of the
homing beacon. I said, 'There's a *housing device* right in
the middle of town.'

'CUT. Okay, let's go back. Keep it together now.'

I don't know why I was feeling under so much pressure.
I had already done my worst scene. It was one that was cut
from the film, in which 888 Thai marching troops passed

in front of what was supposed to be Lon Nol's reviewing
stand. They were real Thai army troops playing
Cambodians, and when the drummer got to my shoulder
I was to be seen leaking information to Sam Waterson.
When the drummer got to my shoulder I missed my cue.
In 110 degrees, 888 troops had to march all the way back.
It took about twenty minutes. Then Sam missed a cue.
Then something went wrong with the camera. It took six
takes, and by the sixth take, far into the day, I saw these
troops coming at me and an insidious voice inside me was
whispering, 'You're going to miss it, you're going to miss it,
you're going to miss it.' Now who is that voice? And what
is that voice? That's all I want to know.

'Okay, boys and girls, let's go. Take sixty-five.'

'A computer malfunction put out the wrong set of co-
ordinates. It seems a single B-52 opened up over Luong …
over Neak … sorry.'

'All right, Spalding. Take sixty-six.'

At last I had the image for the homing beacon. I saw a
pigeon, a homing pigeon, flying towards a lighthouse
beacon in a children's storybook. Got it.

'Let's go. Take sixty-six.'

'A computer malfunction put out the wrong set of co-
ordinates. It seems a single B-52 opened up over Neak
Luong. There's a …' and I knew it would work. It didn't
matter what I was thinking, so long as I was thinking
something. Because everyone looking at the film would be
thinking their own thoughts and projecting them on me.

'There's a homing beacon right in the middle of town.
Check it out, Sid.'

The entire crew burst into applause. Sixty-six takes later
and five hours into the night we had finished the first
scene of the evening. And I was told that it would cost

$30,000 to process it, including the cost of the film and crew. Then, when I got back to New York, I was called in to re-dub the entire scene anyway, because of the sound of crickets. So what you hear in the film is my voice in New York City, reacting to some black-and-white footage shot one hot night on the Gulf of Siam.

Spalding Gray, one of America's master oral storytellers, turned his experience of being in the film *The Killing Fields* into a live solo performance, *Swimming to Cambodia*. In live storytelling, voice is all important, and here, on the page, you can 'hear' Gray's humorous, ironic voice as he ranges over a wide territory, exploring the horrors of war, the way it has become a media event, and his own reactions and failures. His voice is essentially conversational — he is talking to his readers, taking them into his confidence.

WRITING EXERCISES

1. Letters

If you feel your narrating voice is stiff or doesn't 'sound' like you, try writing a chapter as if it were a letter. Imagine a friend or relative with whom you can be most yourself, then start: *Dear Jane/Jim, I want to tell you about* ... Continue on, keeping in mind that you are telling this particular person about the events. Once you feel at ease in the voice, you can leave the letter 'frame' out. *(30 minutes)*

2. Secrets

If you observe that you, as narrator, have become overly careful or cramped by what other people might think of what you are writing, try secret writing. Select an aspect of your memoir where you are most likely to be wary of other people's opinions, then tell yourself that no one will see it, you will not include it in the final manuscript. Begin with the sentence: *I am the only person who will ever see the following, but I need to write it down.* Continue with the complete freedom of knowing there will be no judgment of what you have written. You can write whatever you please, however you please. When you finish, you can even destroy the pages. But before you do, read back over them and see whether the voice has become more honest, whether it has more energy and authenticity. If so, continue writing as if no one will ever read it. You can always edit later if necessary. *(30 minutes)*

3. Journal

Write about an episode from the past — it could be from childhood, adolescence or only a few years ago. The next day, without re-reading the first piece, write the episode again, but this time write it as if in a journal kept at the time of the events. Remember that in your journal you are younger, probably have a more limited vocabulary, have less perspective on events and are probably still emotional about them. Notice whether there is a difference in the closeness or distance of the narrating voice. *(15 minutes for each part of the exercise)*

4. Outside/Inside

Write about a significant episode in your life as if writing an account for a social historian or other researcher who wants to know about this period in your life. Write it as honestly and with as much detail as you can but write from your stored intellectual memory of events. The next day, without re-reading the first piece, immerse yourself in the memory of that time and write it again, in the present tense, as if it were happening right now. Write it as if the memory is going to disappear forever and you need to re-create it as exactly as possible on the page. *(30 minutes for each part of the exercise)*

5. Juggling time

Write five or more different episodes that have happened at different times, but which are connected in terms of the narrative. Use the narrator to connect the various times, directing the reader by using 'locating' phrases. *(At least half a page for each episode)*

5.

MAKING TAPESTRY — TEXTURE AND DETAIL

THERE IS A famous series of six tapestries, *The Lady and the Unicorn*, displayed in the Musée de Cluny, the Museum of the Middle Ages in Paris. They show a medieval lady and her maidservant surrounded by elements of both their natural and cultivated worlds: a bowl of fruit, a small carved chest, a harpsichord, berries, flowers, dogs, rabbits, monkeys, a lion and, of course, a unicorn. Each tapestry represents a sense, the sixth one being love. I have not learned the art of tapestry, but *The Lady and the Unicorn* is one of my teachers, because as well as being a beautiful work in its own right, it reminds me of what I need to do as a writer.

It includes all the senses — and adds love. It shows exquisite attention to detail; it represents the actual world as well as the symbolic world of the mind and spirit with economy and clarity; it revels in colour and texture — indigo, blood red, amber, forest green; it reveals the ordinary elements of life as extraordinary; it shimmers with what is unsayable. A writer's needle and thread is different, but, if you work with the same attention as those unknown tapestry makers, you can create, from the strange silk, cotton, string and wool of words, your own tapestry of marvels.

It begins with attention and observation. All good writing comes from paying attention to — observing — yourself, others, your environment. You know this already, but it is so easy to let your attention become dulled, to become too busy to really notice anything, to become immersed in paying bills, getting to the office, washing up, arranging to go to the dentist. Naturally, writers must earn a living and do these daily chores — probably not many of you have maidservants and unicorns in your lives — but you can do your ordinary activities with attention so that the mind is trained, ready to write, when you sit down. See the bubbles in the washing water, hear the whirr of a bicycle tyre on a wet road. It is a quiet awareness amongst the busyness of life that Buddhists call 'right attention' or 'wakefulness'. It means being properly 'awake', that is, being aware of what you are doing, seeing, feeling, thinking.

How do you wake yourself up? Here are a few possibilities.

- Find time each day, even just a few minutes first thing in the morning, to pay 'right attention' to your immediate environment, to really observe at least an aspect of your world with focused attention, with all your senses. Look at your own hand, listen to the sound of a car horn at night in a quiet street, smell the scent of a freshly opened book. Notice the myriad textures of lived experience. It doesn't have to be beautiful — you may observe a crushed snail. There is as much revelation in an act of violence accurately witnessed as a field of poppies delicately observed. Contemplate the extraordinariness of any blade of grass existing at all. Note down what you see, hear, smell, even for ten minutes of every day. It will reawaken and sharpen your writing mind.

- Go back to a writer who has 'woken you up' in the past. Re-read passages that startle you with their insights and observations — it can be like taking a perception-enhancing potion. For me, Annie Dillard's *Pilgrim at Tinker Creek* is always a refreshing draught. Remind yourself that you have the same capacity to observe your world.
- Seek out an inspiring work from another art form: a powerful painting, a piece of music, a song, a poem, a film — even a tapestry. Immerse yourself in it; give yourself over to another form of expression. Find artists who are 'tearing the veil of habit' that normally drapes itself over life. It might be a singer who wakes you up to the detail of a crumpled dress, or to the sound of a footfall in the passage at three o'clock in the morning. Experiencing art of every genre is one of the best ways to refresh a dull awareness; all kinds of neurones will begin firing and forming new neural pathways in your brain.

Sex and death and the six senses

The smell of a towel warmed by a fire, the sight of redwoods in a Californian valley, the feel of cold air on your cheeks early on a winter morning in a London park — the world is first, and every day, apprehended by the senses. Almost immediately afterwards, you have an emotional response to it. You may then conceptualise what you have experienced, and even philosophise about it, but the fundamental texture of lived experience lies in the sight, touch, sound, smell and taste of the world. To convey what it is like to be in the world, a memoir writer needs to show at least something of that texture. To do that, the writer re-creates the sensory experience — or, at least, uses words to trick the mind into thinking it is receiving information from the senses.

The more overwhelming the experience, the more difficult it can be to find the words to convey it. In intense experiences, such as the meltdown of sex or the devastation of death, the brain typically reacts in a paradoxical mode — senses can be heightened even though the mind feels as if it is floating, or numb. We may see the fly crawling on the curtain as sharply as if a high-powered film light was trained on it, while our brain and emotions feel switched off. Emotions are difficult to write anyway, without becoming too abstract or clichéd, and when the feelings are powerful, words can feel inadequate. It is easy for writing about death, loss and grief to become 'purple' or sentimental, easy for writing about sex and romantic love to become either flowery or uncomfortably explicit. (We all have a different sensibility about this! Some prefer scientific names like labia and testicles, others prefer colloquial names like lips and balls, others again use imagery, likening the sexual organs to a landscape of moist valleys or tangled jungles. The choice depends on the tone you want in your writing.) There are no simple answers, but if you remain as honest as possible with the simplicity of sensory details and images — iron bed, tight sheets, neatly folded tissues, surprising moles dotted along a spine — then you have a chance of conveying some of the texture of lived experience. There is also the importance of spareness, of economy. In writing sex, in particular, it is the 'blow by blow' account that can become either exhibitionistic or just plain embarrassing. A few well-chosen words can give more space for the reader's own imagination, thus making the scene more suggestive and erotic. I suggest that it is both more honest and more powerful to recall the actual body — skin, sweat, freckles, muscles — than either a scientific or a sentimental body.

Words about food can actually make the mouth water; words about a threatening situation can make the heart beat faster; words about sex can create arousal. It strikes me as bordering on sorcery that a system of signs on the page can enter the mind and cause the body to react as if it had received sensory input. I remember, for example, how the vile odours evoked in Patrick Süskind's *Perfume* caused my body to recoil, sickened, as if I was actually smelling the filthy streets of medieval Paris. Of course, *Perfume* is a novel, but as a truthful representation of life, memoir needs to pay the same attention to the sensory world — pleasant and unpleasant. Writing which connects deeply, which makes the reader feel as if he knows and understands, affects the body as well as the emotions and mind. While words shape our experience of being, they can also re-create it in the mind and body.

Writing for the senses is often taken to be seductive, pleasurable writing — the smell of coffee brewing in a sunny kitchen, creamy lilies glowing amongst dark green spears, the silky grace of a baby's cheek — and it is true that sensual writing can reawaken the delights our senses afford us. But the world is also made of the dark, decaying and repulsive: the stench of urine in a dank alley, yellow pus oozing from a child's infected eye, the scream of a woman late at night in the red-light district, the ugly thud of a fist on flesh. This is the lived texture of life; this is what our senses tell us.

The life of the senses is also rhythmic — there is a pulse, a throb, a to-and-fro, which is an intrinsic part of the natural and built world. The rush of waves up the sand and the tugging back, the breath drawn in and let out in a sigh, the thumping of an engine in a shearing shed, the lub-dub pump of the heart muscle — nothing is still. Even stone is weathered rhythmically by the rain and wind. This rhythm can be re-created in the internal rhythm of sentences and the pattern of sentences within paragraphs. Read your words out loud so that you become aware of the rhythm — notice that some sentences are short and jerky, poking a finger at the reader; some are languid and lazy, twirling the reader around a finger; some mimic the movement of speed, sharp and racy, or the dreaminess of a hot summer afternoon, slow and long. The rhythm of sentences is essential to the re-creation of the experience of life. Virginia Woolf stated that for her, rhythm was the first impulse — that if she was blocked it was because she could not find the right rhythm.

Here is a (very) long languid sentence from *Whatever The Gods Do.*

> When I came upon the kite it was already flying long horizontal infinity signs back and forth across the sky. I don't know whether this was a beginning or a bold change of pace halfway through, but then it flew straight up and looped around and back down its vertical path, then glided gently down almost to the lagoon surface before curving upwards and into a sensuous jazzy dance across the top of an imaginary vertical dance floor, rolling and slinking and flirting, joyous and tempting, then suddenly diving in a death-wish straight down to the sand, jerking out of it at the last moment and dancing lazily over the lagoon like a dragonfly skitting and buzzing on a summer's day, playing with light and air, then another long slow climb upwards, nosing this way and that, testing the limits of the upper air before performing long slow arabesques across the top of the sky. It went on and on, intricate and patterned, an airy ballet in the sky.

Feel the contrast in rhythm with the following relatively short, sharp sentences later in the same memoir.

On the shelf over his bed there was a photograph of Dina, her dark eyes sparkling. I sat down on the bed and looked up at it. Theo ignored my gaze.

'Your mum,' I said.

'Yeah.'

'She was beautiful.'

'Yeah.'

I looked at him but he was busy pulling the axle out of a plastic wheel. I looked down at the flowery boots. There was a white smudge on the toe where the flowers had rubbed off.

'These were your mum's.'

Theo looked at the boots briefly and then went on with the axle operation.

'Thought they looked stupid,' he said.

Writing for the senses is not an invitation to excess. It is about creating a convincing world on the page, be it the richly detailed world of a Breughel painting or a spare haiku by the Japanese poet, Basho. In either case there is the desire to convey one's own perceptions of the world. It might be that rich, lush writing suits some writers, but it can be just as valuable to write in an economic, understated style. To a twenty-first century consciousness, too many details can feel heavy, overdone, or simply outdated. You probably don't want your memoir to sound as if it were written in the nineteenth century — unless, of course, you are consciously creating a post-modern reference to nineteenth century literature by using that style.

Still, if you feel your writing is becoming too dry and overly analytical, or if you simply want to build the richness of sensory experience into your writing, try rebuilding the connection between the senses and words.

- Return to the 'original' memory where the details are fresh rather than analysed 'stored' memory. Look for 'madeleines' in your own life. (More on this back in chapter 3, 'The Importance of Madeleines'.)
- Include all the senses, not just sight. Many writers over-rely on sight. Remember the smell, taste, feel and sound of your life.
- Remember colour and texture. Crimson, cream, cobalt; sooty, scratchy, hairy.
- Be accurate about the detail — was it azure or cobalt? Were the leaves serrated or smooth? It is not that you must include every detail — the writing would soon be weighted like someone wearing too much jewellery — but make sure the details are precise.
- Use more sensual rather than abstract words: 'She wore a cream silk blouse and black Chinese trousers' instead of 'She was dressed elegantly'. It helps the reader 'see' it in their mind rather than merely constructing an idea without colour or form.
- Find the particular names of things rather than using general terms; for example, instead of 'a bird flew out of the bush', look more closely, even check in a reference book and write, perhaps, 'a thrush flew out of the japonica'.
- Remember not to overdo it. Too many adjectives and adverbs look like clutter. One effective word can clarify more than a whole row of descriptive adjectives or mod-ifying adverbs. As the American writers Strunk and White said, 'It is seldom necessary to say all.'
- On the other hand, if luscious excess is your preference, do it in style! Taking it to an extreme might be just what is needed. Not all writers need to be restrained and elegant!

- Replace a word of Latin origin with an Anglo-Saxon one. If you are unsure of the difference but suspect your writing may be overly academic or detached, check the origins of some of your characteristic words in a dictionary. Words of Latin origin tend to be more rarified, more academic and cool; Anglo-Saxon words tend to feel more 'earthy' and direct, even for abstract concepts. Try 'truth' instead of 'veracity', 'happen' instead of 'eventuate'.
- Read some poetry. Find Dylan Thomas's *Under Milkwood* and luxuriate in the original imagery and rhythmic delights. Read it out loud. Go back to your own writing with a mind and body buzzing with the richness of the sounds and rhythms of language.

And what about that 'sixth sense', love? Perhaps the tapestry-makers were suggesting that love uses all the senses, rather than it being a sense of its own. Certainly love heightens awareness. Or is it that paying 'right attention' heightens love and compassion? This is, perhaps, venturing too far, making too great a claim for the practice of writing, but it could be that the more accurately and truthfully you try to write your experience of existing, the more your heart opens to the mystery of being in the world.

Many years ago, a friend at art school who was gifted with an extraordinary natural drawing ability said she distrusted 'the lovely line' which she could make easily and impressively. I didn't know what she meant at the time and wondered why she criticised her own ability, but I can see now she meant that such a line is only decorative, that it did not convey any truth. She simply had the ability to make it 'look good'. When you have a facility with writing, it can be easy to write 'the lovely line', to write to impress. The desire to write with beauty can easily be confused with the desire to impress. If you are really ruthless, you will take out every 'lovely line'. How do you tell which ones they are? Look for a certain smoothness, a prideful ease; the sleek swan gliding effortlessly on the still waters of your mind.

Writing for the senses is not decoration, not a pretty painting you hang on the wall to match your carpet. If it is, throw it out. If it is padding to make the writing look or feel more substantial, throw it out. And if it is to make your writing sound more impressive or clever, throw it out. Writing for the senses is not about showing how elegant you look clothed in such fine words.

Writing for the senses is the flesh and the muscle of your writing, as essential as your own flesh and muscle. Every word you write must be necessary. Each one must be there to help construct the illusion of a world on the page. If you are using the senses to create a character, keep it. If you are building mood or atmosphere, keep it. If you are furthering the narrative or exploring an idea, keep it.

Writing for the senses is to acknowledge and celebrate and expose the marvel — or the horror — of anything existing, of letting the ordinary white bowl on the pine table glow with its own reality. Writing for the senses is part of three-dimensional writing, writing which gives the illusion of life-likeness and, at the same time, honours the mystery of existence.

Back to tapestry

To make a textured and life-like 'tapestry', it is worth returning to EM Forster's perennial advice, 'Show, don't tell'. Forster was a novelist, but memoir writers need to create a convincing reality on the page just as much as novelists do. In fact, from a writer's point of view, it doesn't really matter if the reality you are creating is a representation of an actual or imagined world, you still need the reader to believe in it.

Memoir writers often succumb to the pleasure of simply telling their story. In this sense 'telling' means recounting and interpreting events as a historian might: for example, *My father was an authoritative man*. It is a useful way of keeping control of the material and moving the story along and it can be vivid and evocative. At the same time, it only lets one voice be heard, the voice of the teller, and it can result in over-control of the material, over-analysis, and flatness of texture. When this happens, you, as narrator, need to step off stage and let the actors on — you need to 'show' what is happening.

'Show' in this context means creating scenes with a setting, action and dialogue. In a sense, you become more like a playwright, creating the smell and feel and look of the place and characters, letting the reader 'hear' what the people in your life have said, and letting them 'see' what they did. *Shadowy verandah, tall striding man. 'Come here this minute, lad.'* It creates a sense of a three-dimensional world, one that the reader can inhabit — and importantly, it lets readers interpret the scene for themselves, just as they do in life. *He must be in a hurry, or angry. Let's see what he does next.*

Showing a scene makes the experience more believable than if you 'tell' about it because the reader can 'see it with their own eyes'. Stating what you consider to be a truth outright is no guarantee it will be considered convincing. The more times you 'tell' it, the less convincing it can become. In one class, a woman repeated many times in a piece of writing how wonderful her husband was and how much she had loved him. The more she stated it, the less convinced I was. I told her she needed to 'show' me her husband so that I believed that she saw him as wonderful. She went away and came back with a piece about her husband's hands as he played the piano. Then I believed her.

In real life, all you get is what people say and do. There is no tape running along the bottom of life interpreting what is going on. You interpret, you 'read' life all the time. It can actually weaken the impact of an experience to have it interpreted on the page. Let your story speak for itself. Let your readers 'read' your life, rather than telling them what to think and how to feel all the time.

Of course, you might not remember exactly what people said and did. You have a responsibility to the truth as you perceive it, particularly where other people are concerned, but you were not standing there taking notes on your life so you do not have an accurate record. On the other hand, you are not in a court of law when you write a memoir. Remembering the gist of a conversation is enough to re-create it on the page. If you feel uncomfortable 'making up' the conversation, you can always state that this is simply the way you remember it, not the definitive record.

Forster's advice doesn't mean you 'show' everything. It would take too long and become dull anyway. 'Showing' is like a close-up in a film — it gives significance, it reveals something we are meant to pay attention to. *Boots on steps. Creaking boards on the verandah.* It's not so much that you intellectually choose to 'show' one scene and 'tell' another, rather you sense that a particular event in your life would be more engaging, vivid, powerful, if the reader could 'see' and 'hear' it directly, rather than have it recounted as if by a reporter who was there at the time.

Both ways of writing are part of the tapestry. Telling is useful for the overview and for moving across and through time; showing is useful for revealing the moment. Some writers can get away with using just one or the other —

Frank McCourt's *Angela's Ashes* is almost all 'showing', Vladimir Nabokov's *Speak Memory* is almost all 'telling'. They are both successful autobiographies. For most writers, a rhythmic to-and-fro between the two is probably the most effective way of exploring and revealing their experience.

Stitch your tapestry with attention to detail. Even the background is important. Remember colour, shape, movement. *Wire screen door flying wildly, banging shut. Puppy's claws skittering on the hall linoleum.*

READING

Drink Me

by Skye Rogers

I feel as though I know him. This tall, gentle man seems familiar to me — cut, somehow, from the same cloth. My hands regard the slimness of him — slim to the point of fragility. Daniel's muscles are as though chiselled from bone or rock; they are narrow but strong and firm, unyielding. They betray his softness, his yieldingness, the tenderness of those great, padded hands that look like they've been stitched and quilted with satin. He runs them over the length and breadth of me, quite as though I am being discovered for the very first time. I feel every curve and sway and bump as he feels them, the beautiful, powerful land of my body under his hands. I am amazed at how beautiful I feel, how he has made me beautiful. Oh dear, I think, I am in deep already.

In the morning, his long back to me, I note the fragility of Dan's skin on his lower back: it is glowing white, like alabaster, bloodless, the skin of a statue. The breadth of his upper back, his shoulders, though, unlike a statue's, are a page of discolourings: freckles as full stops, moles like question marks, a punctuation of birthmarks. Silently I play join-the-dots until my new friend stirs.

'Shhh, don't wake,' I say. 'Keep sleeping.'

'But I might miss something,' he says, turning over to nudge me under his arm again. I feel my toes make contact with his calves and wonder, momentarily, what it must be like to be so tall, to view the world always from so far above. 'Can't sleep if I'm going to miss anything.'

I smile. Attempting to be funny with a crushing hangover. Now there's a lark.

Daniel's height, the dark, our drunkenness, mean I haven't really seen his eyes.

Still, there will be time to look later.

Instead, I 'see' Daniel, look at and study him, the way I always do with things unfamiliar — I draw and draw until I get him down, give life to his features with my pastels on black paper, my pen and inks on board ...

... The image floats into my mind: Dan reading the paper in his sunny little sitting room — he'd moved some months before into his own place, not far from his parents — trying to placate his worried dad, knowing exactly how to go about it. And then I am visited by the startling vision of him sitting bolt upright by his bed, neat and dead, some hours later. For a moment I think, typical Dan, sitting up so as not to 'miss anything'. I remember all those times I looked in on him in his room, to find him sitting awkwardly with his back up against an array of junk, claiming he was 'cosy as can be'. *I can only hope he was cosy.*

'God bless you, Mary. God bless you.' I have never said

those words before in my life. And then, 'Will there be a funeral?'

A silly question, but it is the kind of moment in which they bloom.

'Well, yes …' A slight pause, no mention of when.

'May I come to the funeral?'

Another thing I hadn't meant to ask. It just came out. I hadn't 'stayed strong' after all. I hadn't been willing or able to go down with the sinking ship. *Perhaps I was not welcome?* I had an innate respect for Mary and Glen in that they had been Dan's parents forever. I was his partner for seven years. Their grief differed from mine, always. Did we love the same man? I wondered. Yes and no. We'd grieve for our own versions of him.

'We'll let you know. We'll probably have something private …'

After hanging up the phone, I crouch to the ground and make a noise so animal that I frighten the dog, that poor beast who is always the first witness to my pain.

The facts simply have to be digested, taken at face value. He is dead. Dan is dead.

Slap, slap, slap. This, another of those days whose reverberating shock renders everything I think I know different, other worldly. I feel tricked, betrayed by the sun still shining in through the windows as though nothing has happened, as though this event isn't even a blip on the universe's radar.

I ring my father who, devastated, has to pull himself together to go back on air in a few minutes. Somehow he gets hold of my mother in those minutes, who comes around straight away, holding me in a mother's embrace for a long, long time. 'What a tragedy,' she says, her eyes brimming with tears. *There but for the grace of God, etc.* I cannot cry. Shock has stolen all my tears.

The airy house feels claustrophobic, so we go for a walk. The sky is too blue, too harsh, any noise an assault. Birds, crisp as ironed handkerchiefs, are fluttering across the sky — handkerchiefs, handkerchiefs everywhere. My senses are a giddy muddle of being shut down and awakened all at once. I am rubbed raw with stimuli, bombarded by life's insistence on continuing its cacophony all around me.

Every inch of this neighbourhood seems to hold a memory of Dan: his friend Gaz in the corner house, DB's 'party house', the park where Rose would annoy him by jumping on his back and the dog would annoy him by being the dog, the pub … The pub I know I won't be able to look at for some time to come. We walk past it with eyes lowered as though this were all its fault, its hops-sweet smell turning my stomach sour.

My mother snaps off a bough of frangipani from a neighbour's front yard — though she doesn't know it, it is the yard of yet another mate from the pub. 'We'll plant this for him,' she says.

We wander the streets aimlessly, the milky sap from the branch leaving a trail behind us like thick, white blood.

In these passages, Skye Rogers reveals that death, too, is experienced through the senses, just as love is. In love or sexual attraction, the senses are intensely awake; in the devastation of loss, our senses are assaulted by ordinary life continuing. Read *Drink Me* for its honest exploration of a relationship in which both Rogers and her partner are battling for a life together, and for the way the pain and the pleasure of their world is evoked through writing the detail of sensory experience.

WRITING EXERCISES

These exercises are more for stimulation and enrichment than for including in your memoir. They are more like a homeopathic dose of Word Essence to stir up your writing self.

1. Senses and emotion

Select an incident in which you experienced strong emotion. Convey the experience without naming it and without using abstract words — no 'grief', 'love', 'anger', 'pity', 'joy'! Evoke the experience through the senses and through 'showing' — action, dialogue and scene. This is an exercise in disciplined writing; it doesn't mean you leave out abstract words forever after. It is a revelation, though, to see how much a good, hardworking, non-intellectual word can do. *(20 minutes)*

2. Cross-fertilising

This is for writers who feel their writing is becoming flat and predictable. Find a CD or interactive encyclopaedia which demonstrates the sound of various musical instruments. Listen to, for example, the sounds of the flute, piano, cello, triangle, oboe. For each one, try to write its colour, texture and taste. Are flute notes pale blue or lime green? Does the sound of an oboe 'feel' like velvet or 'taste' like warm chocolate? Simply write a list of associations that come to mind as you listen. *(20 minutes)*

3. Emotion

Imagine a series of emotions. This means not just thinking about the emotion, but actually feeling it — you will need to think of a specific memory to bring the emotion back — so it can be an exhausting exercise. As you induce each emotion, observe and write down the bodily sensation you experience and any images that come to mind. Recall, for example, confusion, jealousy, anger, joy. It is probably best to end with a positive emotion if you don't want to be left with tight shoulders! *(5 minutes on each emotion)*

4. Novelty

Go somewhere or do something you have never done before. It can be as easy as going to a different part of town and sitting in a new café or listening to a new musician in a pub or eating a new food at a multicultural fair. Note and write the experience from each one of your senses.

5. Action

Make a list of movements — a cat stalking, a leaf blowing, a woman striding, a mouth yawning. Try at least five of the movements, immersing yourself in the sensations. Spend five minutes, for example, as a stalking cat. (It's probably best done when no one is watching.) Note and write the bodily sensations and the images of movement that come to mind. *(5 minutes on each action)*

6. Poets know

Read a poem by a twentieth century poet — your choice of poet, but the poem must be about a person, place, thing or emotion, rather than an intellectual or political idea. Read it slowly, three times. Pick the three words that are most evocative to you. Write three short pieces using each word as a springboard for your own memories. *(5 minutes on each word)*

7. Remembered senses again

Try this exercise from chapter 3 once more. It is a memory exercise but is just as useful in writing for the senses. Write a list of sensory experiences — of smells, tastes, sounds, touches and sights. The list must be very precise — don't write *the smell of roses*, but *the smell of the red rose just inside my grandmother's front gate*. Don't write *the sound of rock music*, but *the sound of Pearl Jam coming from my teenage son's bedroom*. Then select one of the sense memories, concentrate on it and try to find the words to evoke the whole sense experience. *(20 minutes)*

6.

FINDING FORM —
STRUCTURAL
TROUBLESHOOTING

THERE'S AN OLD computer game, one of the earliest, called Tetris, the aim of which is to fit together different shaped blocks as they fall down the screen. That's it. No dragons, no warlords, no commandoes — just irregular shaped blocks falling steadily to be manipulated into place. Nothing else happens. I could watch this game for hours. I don't think I'm especially easily pleased, or especially strange in my pleasures; it's just a simple delight in things fitting together — and 'things fitting together' is a key element of structure.

Watch children — or adults — playing with a jigsaw puzzle: the pleasure they experience when each piece joins, the irritation when a piece will not fit. We humans appear to take an innate delight in fitting one part with another to connect them. This pleasure and delight is the basis of structure, the underlying principle of form. Form is based on pleasure.

It does not mean that everything you write ought to fit snugly or predictably together; you might be making a collage with overlapping pieces rather than a jigsaw, or the spaces between things might be significant; but it does mean there will be a sense of each thing belonging (unity), in that sequence (coherence), and holding together (cohesion).

Of course, you could have all these elements — unity, coherence and cohesion — and simply end up with a box of neatly stacked blocks. You could admire it for a bit, but then it would become uninteresting. There's obviously more to it.

Beauty and truth

There is a beauty of form in the natural world that comes from adapting to the environment to survive. The pencil-like elegance of the poplar is a successful adaptation to the need to conserve water in dry Mediterranean climates; the graceful shape of the panther evolved according to the requirement to be fast and agile. The beauty of both comes from necessity. If, when you are considering the structure of your memoir, you think in terms of what is necessary, you cannot go far wrong. *Be as ruthless as nature when you are considering what needs to be included.*

There are many aspects to beauty. According to a classical philosophy of art, proportion is one of the central require-ments. It sounds a bit formal and eighteenth century — in fact as a philosophical and mathematical idea it goes right back to Aristotle — but all it means is that the various parts of any work of art do not overpower each other. In architecture and the visual arts, ratios such as the famous Golden Mean of $1:1.618$ which, it has been shown, is the basis of proportion in the human body, were used to achieve pleasing proportions. In literature, there is nothing as absolute, because writing tends to be a less prescriptive art, but there is still the need for the various elements to be in proportion. That doesn't mean that memoirs all have to have a neat and pleasant shape, just that the proportions need to support your purpose.

A sense of proportion creates shape, pacing and meaning. Creating a pleasing or exciting or demanding shape depends on all the elements working together, with no one passage or story or character overbalancing the rest and the events unfolding in a way which does not lose or bore the reader. Pacing means that everything unfolds at the 'right' speed — not too slowly, not too quickly. This requires a sensitivity to the emphasis and arrangement of the material. How long or short does a particular passage need to be? Where does it need to go in relation to other pieces? Should this passage go first or should I move it to the middle? Is the unfolding of the story too slow if this piece is included? Have important events been rushed over? Should that paragraph really be a chapter — or the other way around? Will the meaning be changed if I leave it out?

For a memoir or any work of art to be more than pleasingly organised elements, there needs to be a sense that it is going somewhere, that it is about something more engaging than a well-stacked box of blocks, that it has *meaning*. It doesn't necessarily have to have an ongoing narrative (although narrative is probably the most popular structure) but it does need to have a sense that something — meaning — is unfolding. A memoir constructs meaning; it constructs your truth. Changing proportions or emphasis in your memoir will inevitably change your truth. Writing one paragraph on an affair creates a different emphasis from writing a chapter on it. Change proportion and you change meaning.

All the same, meaning is not necessarily a starting point. Beginning with the abstract idea of meaning or themes tends to result in an over-controlled structure — the reader can see the writer running about with the plans. (Of course, you may want to foreground the structure — more on this later.) In both my own writing and in looking at other writers' drafts, I have found that it is better to concentrate on the material itself at first, that is, to start writing the memories without worrying about how to place them.

You don't need to know everything or have it all structured before you start. You write a book not so much because of what you know, but because of what you don't know. You have passionate questions that you want to explore. If you know exactly where you are going and how to get there, the whole incentive of discovery is missing. You would be merely filling in what you already know. If the passionate questions required to write a book have been answered, it makes it hard to start and plodding to write.

On the other hand, if you delay thinking about structure for too long, the whole memoir can become unmanageable and end up shapeless or, at least, very lumpy. A fundamentally flawed structure can be very difficult to undo and sometimes requires starting again.

Rather than trying to work out the whole structure before-hand, or wandering aimlessly along, feel your way in the dark for a while. Be sensitive to what is emerging in your writing. Your memoir might not be about what you first think it is. The creative process has its own agenda, which does not always correlate with the conscious mind's plans. The process of trying things out, of playing, can help reveal what is in the dark.

Feeling the way

This is not a step-by-step list of things to do, because structure does not work that way, but it is a list of ways to feel your way in the dark, ways of playing with possible structures. Try them to find the ones that suit you.

- Instead of sitting and thinking, try writing down your vague thoughts and ideas — unsurprisingly, writers tend to think more effectively on the page! This kind of writing does not have to be well formed. It is simply talking to oneself on the page, wondering and wandering through possibilities. The very act of writing can crystallise what might feel amorphous and unusable.
- Jot notes on everything you think you want to include but without ordering or arranging them. If you start with ordering, it stops the flow. Be disorderly to start with.
- Re-read a memoir you have admired, this time noticing how it is structured. Where does the writer begin? What follows? How does she/he connect sequences? What keeps you reading? How does it conclude? Take notes.
- Again, follow the heat. Write what first excites you, then what next excites you.
- After you have stepped into the flow of the writing, let it wander where it will for a while, but then move back and start observing where it is going. It may be time to do some planning, for example, to decide what the limits of your memoir are — what is part of it and what is not. Perhaps decide on a straightforward chronology — or not.
- Play with chronology. Although it is often useful to write the sequence of events 'as they happened' so that readers find out in the same way that you did, it can be effective to shuffle events. Draw a time line so that you have a good idea of sequence, then perhaps try starting at the end. Or at a hinge — the point where events swung one way rather than another.

- Consider emulating the structure of other ordered elements, such as the pattern of the seasons, or more challengingly, the patterns of chemistry which the Italian writer, Primo Levi, used in *The Periodic Table*. It is a collection of short stories rather than memoir, but the same type of structure could be used in memoir. Or try an everyday pattern, such as the arrangement of rooms in a house. You could move from room to room, telling 'kitchen' stories or 'bedroom' stories and thus build the spaces and shapes of the house, perhaps creating a metaphor of the self.

- Consider using structuring images — common elements of life, such as beds, or tables, or hands, or smiles. You could write a set of pieces about people or places, each time beginning with the same element, such as a smile. It's not a matter of selecting an image and making everything fit, but realising that, for example, what you notice about people is their smile, and using that as an opening image for each piece of writing.

- Consider the structure of other things you make, or other art forms you enjoy. If you make patchwork quilts, consider whether a patchwork structure might suit your memoir. If you enjoy the structure of music, the repetition of motifs might be worth trying.

- Observe closely the structure of a novel or film that you have really enjoyed. Read or watch it a couple of times and note down how scenes follow one another — in what order and to what effect. Try emulating the pattern you observe.

- Consider foregrounding the structure, including your writing process, so that you take the reader with you 'behind the scenes' as you write. The Pompidou Centre in Paris has its structural elements and functions such as a steel framework and air conditioning pipes on the outside of the building. In a similar fashion you could include some of the 'behind the scenes' writing decisions in the text. You could admit to your readers, for example, that you are weighing up several scenes to decide which will give the right impression. The main structuring element thus becomes the narrator as conductor of stories. In *The Last One Who Remembers*, the narrator was symbolised as a bowerbird because it struck me that a bowerbird collects and puts things together in much the same way as a memoirist. Early in the book, I introduce the bowerbird:

My stories are of varying textures, like a patchwork quilt. Or like the bower of a bowerbird, less straight-edged, less connected than a quilt. A bower is made in a clearing in the undergrowth and shells and cicada husks and feathers and ribbons and pieces of broken willow-ware plates are placed within it. But if I were the bowerbird, the patchwork quilt left out in the backyard might also be plundered and its pieces lain irregularly on the sticks of the bower: velvet and satin and silk pieces in curious fictional shapes, everyday cottons of family gossip, rice papers inscribed with prayers, bark paintings of mythic tales, lacy fragments of memory, starched pieces of sermon and analysis, silvery thread and bone of learned argument.

Then, throughout the memoir, the bowerbird 'flaps' in and out with various pieces, acting as both a structuring image and a device for foregrounding what the narrator is up to in offering these stories.

- Think outside the chapter. Sometimes, smaller units might work better, especially when the memoir is made up of many small events. Rather than trying to force them to conglomerate into a chapter, try them as small pieces that you can move about like pieces of a mosaic.

- If you have many different times or episodes to write about, try a 'frame'. It is a strong structural device for connecting pieces which might otherwise become 'bitsy'. You could, for example, include references to the actual room, house, neighbourhood in which you are writing as a re-occurring device to hold the various pieces together. In *Whatever The Gods Do* I used the time and place of the beach-house where I was staying as a structural frame to hold together the diverse times and places in the memoir.

- Try writing a full-length memoir as a series of short stories rather than as chapters. I don't mean for you to fictionalise your life but simply to construct each story as self-contained, each one complementing the others but able to be read alone as well.

- Explore the plots of traditional narratives — fairy stories and folktales from your own or other cultures. Perhaps you will find the shape of your story in a Russian folktale or a Celtic myth. (If you are interested in this idea, it is explored in more depth in the next chapter.)

- Remember beauty. Beauty of form is created when structure and content are one — when the patterns of the structure echo the material and its meaning. For example, if you are writing about a fragmentary life, then a formal structure of fragments may be necessary and beautiful. If you feel the story you want to tell is circular, then a circular structure — the ending echoing the beginning — may be best.

- Finally, stop planning and start writing. It is easy to become addicted to taking notes, working things out. If the planning becomes too detailed there is a danger the desire to write the memoir will be satisfied by the plan. Allow the material to find its own organic structure.

What goes wrong and how to avoid it

A first draft is really an experiment with structure. Structure is essentially created by the selection, ordering and emphasis of material. In memoir, it is the memories (and perhaps the research) selected, the order in which you arrange them, and the way in which you highlight or shade each one. You cannot know until you have tried it whether it will work or not. Still, there are a number of difficulties that might be avoided or lessened if you know about them beforehand. All of the following issues occur frequently in the manuscripts that arrive on my desk.

- *A 'baggy' structure with too much irrelevant material.* As the *New York Times* columnist, Russell Baker, said, 'just because something happened is not a good enough excuse to write about it'. You need to discriminate between what you have included merely because it happened, and what is included because it relates to your story and themes. Read through your draft asking yourself with each episode, why is this scene included? Does it contribute to what this memoir is about, or have I just put it in because it happened? Be ruthless regarding what is necessary. At this stage, you need to be in charge of your material rather than it being in charge of you.
- *A disjointed structure resulting from mixing topics and narrative.* Some story-based memoirs that also involve significant social, psychological or cultural issues try to combine a chronological narrative with topics — for example, part

of the story of a marriage break-up is told and then there
might be a chapter on the nature of depression. The two
organising principles — narrative and topics — rarely
work together. Choose one or the other. If you need to
have both, then use them in a rhythmic way, moving
back and forth between the two and without repeating
material in both strands.

- *A lumpy structure in which some events are given disproportion-
ate space.* This problem may result from the 'just because
it happened' inclusion, but also because the events are
unresolved in the writer's life. It can lead to avoidance, or
the issue being unduly minimised, or, on the other hand,
obsessive overemphasis. The event/s probably need to be
included, but given more or less space. Perhaps the argument with your mother needs to be mentioned, but not
given five pages. Memoir is not autobiography — you can
be much more selective about what you include and how
much weight you give events. At times, a particularly
emotional and intense passage can unbalance a whole
manuscript. You might need to expand it, and related
passages, to put it in context — or you might need to
leave it out altogether.

- *Parallel story strands which become tangled — and/or the
threads are mismatched.* Two or three story strands weaving
in and out of one another can be a very effective device;
for example, your trip to Greece could be interwoven
with your childhood in a Greek-Australian community in
Melbourne. Problems arise when one strand is more
powerful or interesting than the other, or when there is
repetition of ideas in each strand, or when the links
between the two strands are arbitrary or forced. If you are
weaving together two or three strands, make sure that they
are all significant, that you are not repeating in slightly

different words the same issues, and that they relate to each other in organic ways.

- *A confusing or jumpy narrative structure.* When you are close up to a story it can often be difficult to see if you have all the elements you need — and in the right order — for the reader to follow the story. If you jump about too much without any discernible connection between pieces, the reader can find it too difficult to follow and very easy to put down.

  You can also make the mistake of telling the reader too much, too soon. It can lessen the impact of events if you have pre-empted them — for example, you let slip that you marry Sam when the reader has been turning the pages to find out 'will she/won't she?'

  To avoid leaving out important elements, or pre-empting them, or putting them in a jumpy or disconnected order, it can be useful to draw out a time line of events. For events in which the time sequence is crucial, it is a good idea to maintain a simple chronology, at least in the first draft. If the time sequence is less important or you want a sense of the layering of life rather than a temporal unfolding, then you will need to find ways, such as images and themes, to connect your pieces.

- *A structure that does not seem to hold up, doesn't seem to be going anywhere.* The principal question underlying structure is 'why?' Why are you are writing this, and why are we reading it? Whether stated or unstated, the 'why' of any memoir needs to be set up early and continued throughout, keeping the reader in the story. It is what the memoir is about. If it is not there, or is not justified by the material that follows, then the reader loses the sense that the memoir is 'going somewhere' — and stops reading.

  It is time to step back from the writing, read it through

in as detached a manner as possible — or ask someone whom you can trust with structure to read it — and try to see the underlying story and/or patterns. Decide what needs cutting, or adding, or shifting. Sometimes it might be a matter of a different beginning to allow all the other pieces to make sense. Sometimes it might be that the 'why' you have set up is not true, for example, you may have thought it was about alcoholism but it was really about growing up in a home where the parents did not like one another. It is often the case that a writer has not seen what the material is really about in the first draft. It is the nature of the creative process — the slow emergence of truth.

- *Jerky changes in perspective and pacing in the structure.* Parts of your memoir may be an overview or summarising of several years or of a place or person, while other parts will be close-ups of particular times. This shift in perspective also affects the pacing and the reader's sense of closeness. If it is not done well, the move between the two perspectives can result in the reader feeling dislocated. There is also a danger of repetition of material when you overview, then show a close-up as well. Check to see whether both perspectives are necessary — it might be that one can be deleted, tightening the structure.

In the beginning and the end, structure is a way through for the reader. Whether you stick to the road or lead them on a merry dance through the woods, the reader still needs to feel that you do know where you are going and why. You do not need to know in the first draft — if you can see the entire shape of the journey before you start, there may be no need to write it — but by the time the memoir reaches the reader, there needs to be a sense that it is going somewhere — and that you know how to get there.

Structure can take time and patience. Underneath the efficient mind there is another, darker, dimmer mind that cannot even tie a shoelace — but it does know how a story works. Not that it could tell you how, because it cannot explain anything logically, it cannot argue a point, or defend a case. It does try to make itself heard and seen in daily life but because I (we all) lack the time or the quietness to see the connections, it comes across as confused and incoherent.

This dark mind seems to be made of infinite multi-coloured patterns of physical and emotional memory, insights, sensations, even dreams, flamboyantly filed in its own intricate labyrinthine structure where everything is connected to everything else — not by logic, but by poetic association. It's at the point when the rational organising mind gives up that a writer — or anyone who demands the time and quietness — enters that dark mind. There one writes memoir, paints pictures, finds theorems, designs a new object, rediscovers childhood, realises one has been on the wrong track, sees how change can be made. Afterwards, of course, there are still bills to be paid and chores to be done — but something new has found form.

READING

Whatever The Gods Do

by Patti Miller

About Blood (i)

Some nights over the years when Theo was staying, he had nosebleeds. He would start crying quietly and Mani, who still shared his room with Theo, would yell out, 'Mu–um! Theo's bleeding.' Theo never cried out loud, never drew attention to himself except in passive, self-punishing ways.

I'd come running in and there would be blood smeared and dripping down Theo's face and pyjamas and on the sheets; tears dripping silently over his so-pale cheeks. I would be nearly dancing about with the horror of it, blood vessels breaking, blood surging where it shouldn't, the absurd bright redness of it — who'd have thought there was so much blood in the little boy — my heart pumping in awful recognition, but at the same time, I was very calm. I'd get ice and hankies, cuddle Theo's trembling body, find some old pyjamas of my son's and change Theo — rolling back too-long sleeves — find clean sheets, strip and remake the bed, soak the sheets in cold water.

After both boys were tucked back in, foreheads stroked, cheeks kissed, I'd sit down feeling strained and a bit queasy. Sometimes I'd ring my mother, who had been a nurse, and talk about it. 'Better a nosebleed than anywhere else,' she'd say, and we'd both be silent a little longer than was comfortable.

About Blood (ii)

A Maltese woman in the writing class said that she loved to walk around the house singing opera at the top of her voice, 'Because opera is controlled screaming.' She was a beautiful woman with a twelve year old daughter as beautiful as she was. She once said that if anyone harmed her daughter she would kill them; she would cut their throat. She said it in a way that you knew she meant it — she would actually find and kill anyone who harmed her child. I don't think she was bloodthirsty but she was the only woman I had ever met who has sworn to spill another's blood if the circumstances arose.

About Blood (iii)

Michel read his story carefully, trying to make sure his English was clear. He was a boy of eleven on an Algerian wharf during the war for independence. Hundreds of French-Algerians were milling about on the wharf, all trying to get on boats of any kind to escape across the Mediterranean. There was noise and urgency and Michel had no idea where his mother was. An Arab-Algerian arrived on the wharf and suddenly the frantic atmosphere changed in a menacing way.

Rumour was the Arab had been involved in smuggling guns, probably for both sides, and he too had to escape the rebel Arabs. But he had leapt into the fire. The boy watched the crowd as it metamorphosed into a mob and gathered around the Arab, crying, 'Traitor, traitor.'

A large woman pushed the Arab on the shoulder and he stumbled a little, pleading, 'Leave me in peace. For the love of God.' A weedy man was aroused to shove the Arab in the face, hissing, 'Leech, leech.' The boy's heart beat fast. He recognised mortal fear in the man's eyes, although he had never seen it before.

Someone noticed the boy in front of the crowd and pushed him away. Hands bundled him backwards until he couldn't see the Arab at all. He tripped and fell heavily on the wooden planks of the wharf. There was a horrible cry, 'Mon Dieu, mon Dieu,' which gurgled and choked at the end. Michel saw a bloody knife with a beautifully carved handle thrown down through the forest of legs and he watched it skitter across the planks and disappear under a coil of rope. The mob moved as one to the edge of the wharf, then there was a loud splash as something heavy was heaved into the sea. Michel saw nothing, except where the knife had gone. In a few minutes, unnoticed, he crawled across and reached under the rope.

The writing group sat, pens in hand, ashamed of pallid suburban childhoods. Michel reached into his pocket and pulled out a knife with a beautifully carved handle and put it on the carpet in front of his chair. I stared at it, somehow surprised that it had no blood on it.

About Blood (iv)

Over the summer Theo left, I brewed the Chinese herbs in the kitchen every evening. The herbs were said to increase 'blood energy'. (In western medicine I guessed it must be to do with stimulating hormones to encourage menstruation and libido, but 'blood energy' sounded accurate enough.) The process was something of a ritual and I felt like one of the weird sisters in *Macbeth* — flapping clothes, wild red hair, bat's wings, eye of newt — it made the flesh on my skull creep.

I peered into the brown paper bag of herbs first, a thrill pulsing somewhere. There seemed to be a recognition, a memory, at the sight of the dried fungi, the sticks and leaves and roots mixed together in the bag. There were black rubbery licorice-smelling slices too, and little white chunks of something that looked like dried tofu. I tipped the lot into a Chinese pot — it was a blackened ceramic pot with a spout and handle on either side like two stumpy uplifted arms — then I added three and a half cups of water and put the pot on the gas stove (it needed a little fire of sticks and heather, a dim hut, a spell or two). The first time, Theo was still there and he watched me, fascinated and a little suspicious. The pot steamed away on the stove for more than an hour, filling the house with an acrid, evil smell. Anthony complained, saying it made the place smell like a witch's den. I said, at least he didn't have to drink it. The mixture brewed down to a single cup of thick black potion that tasted even worse than it smelt and caused an involuntary shudder as I sipped it. I felt as if I was drinking black blood.

This memoir, *Whatever The Gods Do*, in part tells the story of a friend of mine who died of a brain haemorrhage — hence the significance of blood in this sequence. The whole memoir is made of many pieces of varying lengths, which are placed in relation to one another, via narrative, theme or image. Here it is the image of blood, but also the theme of transformation. This was structured not according to conscious decisions, but by following the patterns and images which arose as I wrote.

WRITING EXERCISES

1. Scenes in a relationship

Write five separate scenes in a relationship, past or present, in chronological order. It can be a relationship with anyone — mother, sister, lover, friend. The scenes must be self-contained, not referring to any of the other scenes, and each one should be no more than a page. The time between scenes can be anything from a few minutes to many years. Now rearrange them backwards, so that the story begins with the one that happened last. Note how that affects the structure. Try writing five more scenes in the same relationship and fitting them in the sequence you already have. Shuffle them about until you have the most effective structure. *(15 minutes for each scene)*

2. Series of beds

Call to mind beds in your life. Write a series of pieces, at least 1000 words each, using the memories evoked in relation to at least five different beds. Consider a wide range — a childhood bed, a boarding school bed, a lover's bed, a great aunt's bed, a hospital bed, a deathbed, a bed in a tent, a bed in a country motel. As you read back through them, see whether the idea of 'bed' holds them together.

You can also do the same exercise with another piece of common furniture, such as the table. Tables are very productive of memories as they connect to so many things in life — food, family, friendship, romance, arguments, study, work. But don't start writing about any of those topics — go into your memory via a specific table. You can obviously use this exercise with any kind of furniture. Consider whether you might be able to use this idea of a series around a certain object to structure a whole memoir. *(15 minutes for each piece)*

3. Exploring images

Begin with the sentence *I think this memoir is a ...* and insert an image such as a star, journey, treasure hunt, jigsaw puzzle, mountain, river, *because ...* then continue on with teasing out the likeness. For example, *I think this memoir is a river because the story I want to tell begins as a tiny stream and there are many loops and bends. Then, as it gets bigger, there are dangerous rapids and occasional periods of calm flow before the high restrictive banks are reached ...* and so on. This is a way of exploring image-based structure rather than a concept or logical plan. The aim is not to produce a fine piece of writing, but to play with the possibilities of structure. *(20 minutes)*

4. Long and short of it

Write two related episodes you have decided you want to include in your memoir. It might be two scenes from your year in Kenya or two scenes in your life with your disabled son, for example. Write one in half a page, the other in at least three pages. The next day, write the same two episodes, this time swapping the length of the pieces. Note the varying impact and weight that the scenes have at different lengths and how it changes the relationship between the two pieces. (*1 hour each time*)

7.

THE MAGIC SPELL
— NARRATIVE

THE SPELL OF narrative saved Scheherazade's life. She was a beautiful young woman who lived with her father, the Caliph. One day she was sent for by the King. She had to think quickly; the King was in the habit of calling for a virgin each evening and next morning having her killed so that he could be sure he would not be cuckolded. (The King clearly had his problems but let's not go into his story.) Scheherazade's father told her the King liked stories, so, that evening at the palace, she settled herself on the cushions and began to tell him a fabulous story. She continued the story through the night and, in the morning, stopped before the tale was finished. The King, of course, had to keep her alive so that she would finish the story. He had to know what happened next. The following night she continued on with the story and began another, again stopping at dawn before it was complete. Again, the King had to know how things turned out and spared her life. In this way, night after night for one thousand and one nights, she kept herself alive — and the King tantalised. Finally he married her so that she would keep telling him stories and they lived happily ever after.

The story of Scheherazade is, of course, the frame for the *Thousand and One Arabian Nights*, one of the world's most famous collections of folktales, but it is also an allegory of the irresistible attraction of narrative — and its capacity to heal and to save both the teller and the hearer. It seems to me that this capacity comes from the fact that, within a narrative, the random fragments of life are connected to create a meaningful, continuous whole. If one has had an overwhelming experience, the mind either shuts it out or goes over it obsessively, trying to come to terms with it. Writing the narrative or story takes it out of the mind and onto the page where it can be connected to other elements of life. The fundamental nature of narrative is to make causal links between things — in other words, to show that things happen for a reason, that they make sense. Narrative, then, by its very nature, is integrating. By making the links between events, narrative helps us understand — and as the philosopher Spinoza remarked, 'To understand something is to be delivered of it'.

But narratives are also told of the joyful and remarkable events of life. They are told to celebrate, to acknowledge, to remember, to weave community, to persuade, to create beauty, to make meaning. I would go so far as to say that a meaningful narrative is necessary to human life. Without a story, it becomes impossible to act. Why get up in the morning if you do not have a convincing inner story that says this is a worthwhile thing to do?

Story or narrative is also, as Scheherazade knew, immensely attractive. A mediocre novel or film can hold attention because of the narrative alone. Few people can resist an 'addiction' to narrative; it is one of the most powerful human structures. There is an expectation, perhaps formed in earliest childhood from the stories read to us, that all the elements introduced will unfold and connect and come to some kind of satisfying conclusion.

What is narrative, exactly?

Narrative, or story, is simply a way of arranging information or material to create the desire to find out what happens next. This desire is created by narrative pull or narrative tension. It is based on a pattern of withholding and giving information in an enticing fashion — like drawing a bird along a path with bits of bread. If you want the reader to follow you in a certain direction, then the 'breadcrumbs' need to be spaced out, but not so far apart that the reader loses interest and flies off. In the case of stories, they also have to be laid out in an unfolding order, not a jumbled pile, and they have to appear to be going somewhere, preferably not around in circles.

This might seem like manipulating your reader — and some narratives are manipulative. I don't enjoy a narrative when I can sense information is being deliberately withheld for too long. To me, the best memoir narratives are the ones that appear to unfold 'naturally', meaning that the reader finds something out at the same time as the writer appears to.

You might see that your memoir has an overall narrative, and start plotting its structure. This simply means making a chart of the main narrative points in the order that you want them to unfold. For example: *telephone call saying your husband has lost his job in Los Angeles → weeks of despair → decision to sell the house → decision to buy a boat and set sail → violent storm at sea → arriving in Hawaii → beginning of a new life.* Of course, there are any number of ways that one narrative can be plotted (plot being the order and emphasis of the narrative elements). You could decide to start in the middle of the storm, then, leaving your readers dangling, jump back to the telephone call and recount the various plot points that eventually bring the reader back to the storm.

None of this is to say that a good memoir *must* have a strong overall narrative. You might prefer a meditation on ideas, where you are walking back and forth over a terrain rather than a linear narrative. In such a structure, however, there is normally a narrative of ideas, the unfolding of insights and thoughts. Look at Annie Dillard's Pulitzer prize-winning *Pilgrim at Tinker Creek*, in which, on the surface, very little happens. There is no action, adventure or romance in the usual meaning of the words; there is no violent childhood or broken heart, no fabulous journey to an exotic place. It consists simply of observations of nature and, thus, of life, centred on an American creek, yet it is one of the most absorbing and beautiful memoirs I have read.

Alternatively, consider whether a series of narratives suits your material better. If you cannot see that there is an overall narrative then it is best not to force one. A series of short stories might be more effective. If your story is about your life on a cattle ranch in Texas or a sheep farm in New Zealand, then a set of stories evoking the landscape, people, animals and way of life might be effective. Each story could be self-contained, a complete story on its own, while building up an overall picture of Texan — or New Zealand — farm life.

Or you might want to write a set of stories around a single image as English chef Nigel Slater did in his memoir *Toast*. It consists of many short narratives, some only half a page, each one centred around food. He tells the story of his childhood and young manhood, but it is not a conventional continuous narrative. It tells the story of his life in relation to food, and because food is a constant factor in life, he is able to recount all his major experiences through this one topic. A forward-moving narrative is created piece by piece, held together by food being grown, prepared, eaten, shared.

You could also use a series of short narratives which combine to build up an ongoing central narrative using a series of themes. In *Whatever The Gods Do*, I used many short pieces which, together, built several ongoing narratives around the central theme of transformation. I did not begin with the theme — it did not emerge until the final draft — but with the desire to tell the stories as honestly as I could.

Whether you want to write a strong central story or a series of stories, how do you construct narrative out of the shapelessness of life? Start by reminding yourself that you already know how to construct a narrative. It may be difficult to accept that you innately know how to do something as complex as construct a narrative out of the thousands of elements of your life, but it is in fact something that all humans do every day. You automatically sift and sort and arrange the events that happen to you each day — and if you get the chance, you recount those events as a narrative to friends and family. And then, each night as you sleep, your unconscious, your dream self, constructs more narratives, even if they are bizarre and unlikely.

Narrative is natural. All human beings tell stories. Some might argue it is a cultural construction — and its various forms undoubtedly are constructed — but the urge to make a narrative out of what has happened appears innate. Still, when you sit down to write a narrative, it can be difficult to trust that storytelling ability.

It is important not to be overwhelmed by techniques or

instructions on how to do it. If you were writing a detective story or a thriller, then yes, you would have to plot in a detailed way. But with memoir writing it is not so much a controlled intellectual process as one that happens under the surface. The millions of neurones in the brain are already going about their business of making connections between things. It's their job. Sit quietly for a while, hold the elements of the story in your mind and they will gradually find their place. It is often a matter of feeling your way, piece by piece.

Some people are at ease with this process and it flows naturally. For others, here are a few tips. They are not intended to be things you must do, or step-by-step instructions, but simply a few suggestions to try when you feel unable to begin or move forward, or feel that you have lost the track. Some of the advice not only sounds contradictory, it *is* — that's because everyone's approach is different. We don't all need the same advice. You will see what suits you.

A few tips on making a narrative

- Sit quietly, letting events play over in your mind, then begin jotting them down in any order. When you think you have all the elements, start arranging them in a coherent sequence. You don't have to start at the beginning — you can start, for example, at a key turning point — but remember the reader needs to be able to move between times and events without confusion. Often, when you are first starting out, a chronological approach is best.
- Remember the question. At or near the beginning, a narrative needs an unanswered question, or a series of unanswered questions. It is not an openly stated question, but one that ought to form in the mind of the reader.

- If you are clear about the story line, select only those elements of your life that contribute to the narrative. Don't include the visit to Brighton Pier in your 'year in England' memoir if it does not contribute to the story.
- Let there be light — and shade. If you give everything the same emphasis, the narrative will become flat. Some incidents deserve to be written about at greater length and with more intensity than others.
- Include enough information — be aware the reader does not know what you know. Too many gaps and the reader will fall through.
- On the other hand, you don't need to spell everything out. Readers like to make a few leaps of their own. It can be very tedious to be told everything — let the reader make connections sometimes.
- Withhold. You don't have to spill the beans on the first page. Because you recount the story from the perspective of knowing what has happened, you may be tempted to tell everything you know right away — but hold back. Sense the right moment for information to be revealed.
- Don't withhold too much. Holding back information can just feel manipulative and annoying. Teasers and cliffhangers are mostly corny.
- Maintain the narrative tension. Be aware of not pre-empting important narrative points. If you let slip that your son became a surgeon while you are writing the scene where he is lost in the mountains of Colorado, then the narrative tension is loosened.
- Remember pacing. Sometimes you might need to slow down the unfolding events — write more on each event rather than recounting the affair, divorce and remarriage in two pages. Or sometimes you might need to speed up, not spend quite so much time on the end of the affair.

- Remember the pleasure of a narrative of ideas. An inner journey of the unfolding of the self in relation to the world, or the story of an idea, can be very engaging. For example, Lucinda Holdforth's *True Pleasures* unfolds the idea of Paris as a city which supports and nourishes women.
- Think of good narrative as akin to good sex. Seduce your reader by tempting them into your story. Awaken their desire to keep reading, and satisfy their need to find out. Try not to be too predictable, or too slick, or too fast — or too slow.
- Be truthful to the essential shape of the story that has formed or is forming under the surface of your mind. Don't tempt or seduce if that does not fit the integrity of your story — it will only seem forced or artificial.
- Re-read narratives you have enjoyed in memoir, fiction and folk and fairytales and see how the narrative unfolds. The latter are fundamental story-shapes and have formed many people's sense of how a narrative unfolds.

Myths and fairytales

In all cultures and religions there are folktales, fairytales, myths and legends handed down over hundreds, if not thousands of years. These are the narratives that make sense of the elements of life, explaining the natural and human world and celebrating important events and characters. It could be said that they are the archetypes for all our stories. Because these story-shapes have endured for so long, it may be worth looking at them more closely to see whether they might be useful for writing the narrative of a memoir.

There are many researchers, such as Joseph Campbell, who have written at length on the story structures of myths and fairytales. One of the key structures which has been described is the quest myth. It has a three-part structure: departure, initiation, return. Departure involves a sign that something is about to change and often includes a gift of some kind, a talisman from an elder or even an animal. Initiation involves a journey and struggle against difficulties or temptations, but also, regularly, another gift or assistance of some kind — a magic spell perhaps. Return involves the resumption of what might look like the old life, but it is a life transformed, or at least renewed.

It is easy to see how the quest myth structure might echo the pattern of many life experiences, from a sequence of events as terrible as the death of someone loved, to events as light-hearted as sailing around the Mediterranean. If a quest structure appears to fit your memoir, then use those divisions and that shape as a way of organising your material. You don't have to foreground it, or even mention it if you don't want to, but use it as your organising principle. If you are interested in this idea, *The Gift of Stories* by Robert Atkinson explores mythic structures in detail.

Look also at other fairytale structures. Remember the fairytales and folktales from your own childhood. Recall particularly those stories that either delighted or horrified you. It is remarkable how, most often, the tale that makes an impression, either positive or negative, contains an important personal theme, the story symbolically echoing a key story in an individual's own life. For example, for one woman in writing class, the folktale of 'The Man, the Boy and the Donkey' had always horrified her as a child. The essence of this tale is that the man listens to conflicting advice about how to travel with the boy and the donkey, changing his actions with each new piece of advice. Eventually, as a direct result of him trying to please everyone, the man, the boy and the donkey fall off a bridge and drown. After exploring this folktale in relation to her own life, it was clear to this woman that she had lived too much of her life trying to please others, rather than working out for herself the best course of action. This insight helped her select which incidents to tell and which ones to emphasise. It gave her the shape of her story.

Re-read fairytales and folk stories looking at the shared or common narrative points, objects, landscapes and characters. You will notice there are many recurring motifs which can be seen to represent events and people in daily life.

- Narrative points include such life events as loss of a parent, introduction of an evil force, denial of rightful inheritance, banishment, a contest for love, a journey. These are as much a part of ordinary life as of lives in fairy stories.
- Objects such as wands, caskets, shoes (glass slippers?), talismans and amulets, thorns, spinning wheels. In your own life, these objects might correspond with talents, gifts from others, burdens, enticements.
- Landscapes such as mountains, dark woods, swamps, paths, mazes, caves, towers. It is easy enough to see how one can see these symbolic landscapes in ordinary life!
- Characters such as witches and wizards, dragons, wolves, tricksters, stepmothers. Again, these symbolic characters are easily recognisable.

Consider what each element might symbolise and see whether your story contains the same elements. You can use these correspondences in a number of ways, such as selecting a fairytale to use as a prologue for your story, or using elements such as objects or landscapes as chapter titles, or simply keeping the tale and its elements in mind as a shaping device underneath your writing without necessarily mentioning it.

My journey

The first draft of my manuscript, *Whatever The Gods Do*, was a misshapen creature. It had begun as notes on singing lessons I took one summer, but I had no idea where the narrative was going. The death of a friend of mine, and the life of her young son, crept into the notes so that there were two narrative strands. Memories from childhood surfaced — another strand, but more thematic than narrative. My father had died around the same time as my friend — a connecting theme of death. My body was changing according to a biological cycle — another thematic strand. I didn't know how they were linked. I tried to force them together into bulky chapters. It didn't work.

Time and solitude were necessary to sort it out. I took the manuscript away to a beach-house for a few weeks alone. There I read through the whole draft and all my notes for it — and sat and stared at the lagoon at the bottom of the garden. I realised I had to throw away over half of the draft and rewrite and restructure.

I spread the manuscript all over the bed in separate chapters, made notes on cards of the different elements of the stories and themes, drew long charts of the narrative development. I rearranged the chapters, shuffled the cards, put the chart aside. Days passed as I wrestled with it.

On the thirteenth day I wrote in my journal: 'Disastrous day. I've lost all sense of being able to save this manuscript. It would be easier to start from scratch.'

The next entry was two days later:

I have started to play with the ms. I have abandoned the notion of long continuous chapters and let the small pieces exist as they are. Something falls into place. Even this beach-house has become part of the process. A frame. I can see that all the narrative strands are about transformations — some slow and underground, some instantaneous and horrifying. The manuscript feels lighter and suddenly I know I am dancing with it, not boorishly pushing and shoving it. And it starts to respond — it starts to dance with me — pieces are lightly falling into place by beat, by rhythm, as if I were writing a song. It has never happened before — it's a feeling like no other. The narratives are intertwining and moving forward — I think of it as a piece of music, many different instruments playing at once.

As you can see, I tried hard to control the story, to force narrative links, but it didn't work. Narrative is like that. It has its own mind and, despite the best efforts of the intellect, the story it wants to tell will eventually out. You have to give in to its demands. It is a joyful process, the telling of stories, and only becomes difficult if it is too controlled.

Trust that the story is already there. The Renaissance artist Michelangelo said that when he approached his block of marble, he started by trusting that the form of the sculpture was already in the stone. What he was actually trusting was that the shape was already in his mind. It was simply up to him to chip away the unnecessary thoughts that had collected around it. Trust that somewhere in your mind the story is known and set to work, writing down what is necessary, leaving out what is not.

READING

Forever Today

by Deborah Wearing

That Sunday, 10th March, I proposed fresh air, a walk after lunch. Clive did not want to go.

'You'll feel better,' I said.

'I doubt it,' he said.

But I could not let the storm brew any blacker. We had to get outside, to move, to breathe.

'Look,' I said, 'let's drive to Hampstead Heath. If you don't perk up, we'll come straight home.'

He was too poorly to argue.

We parked in a red sandy car park full of potholes.

'It's about to rain,' said Clive.

'Not yet,' I said.

My optimism was at odds with the gathering gloom above our heads.

'Come on, love,' I said, 'let's just walk to Jack Straw's Castle and back, stretch our legs.'

The heath at this north edge made a kind of low mound. I thought we could at least duck into the pub if the rain started. We held onto each other as we always did but the rough terrain was throwing us somehow out of step. Clive stomped, kicking up tufts. He said little. It was as if we had to press against invisible forces to make any ground at all.

We had reached the middle of this expanse of stubbled green when a low rumble filled the sky. We stopped. A double crack split the air above our heads and a cold rain was upon us. We turned, heads bowed. Thunder rolled across the sky. The noise was everywhere, like a fury held in too long, unleashed. The sky pelted us with bullets of ice, stinging our faces. We ran, arms over our heads, all the way back to the muddy car park where the potholes had become puddles bubbling and splashing high into the air where the hail struck. I fumbled with the keys and we got into our car, slamming the doors. It was shelter, but it didn't feel safe. A curtain of white rain surrounded us and sheet lightning lit up the heath. We sat puffing and steaming up the windows. The hail drummed so hard on the roof, I expected dents. Stones bounced high off the bonnet and off the ground. It was a good five minutes before we could see to drive home. The streets were awash with fast-running streams. Waters swelled around clogged drains and our wheels sent up a wave to left and right. It was raining like it would never stop.

The rain had washed our windows clean. I fetched the ironing. It towered above my head as I walked. I must have looked like a stack of laundry on legs. Clive sighed.

'So much?' he said. 'We mustn't let it get this bad.'

'We've not been here,' I said. 'Mind if I switch on the telly?'

'Has the lightning stopped?'

I watched the window for a moment. It was dark outside like twilight, though still only three.

'Uh ... think so.'

'I can't cope with a film or anything with a plot,' he said. 'My head aches.'

I fetched an aspirin and put the sport on low. At some point, Clive left the room and then came back.

The iron bubbled and spat, burning the back of my hands. Another bubbling sound. I looked behind me. Clive was perched awkwardly on top of the laundry, mouth

open, eyes shut, head back. His feet barely touched the
ground. He lay at an angle as if he'd fallen from a height.

'Darling!' I called out.

He opened his eyes and looked across at me.

'Why are you there?' I asked.

'I don't know,' he said. 'I must have been asleep.'

'Go to bed properly,' I said.

I took his hand and led him into the bedroom. He
seemed lost and sleepy so I undid his buttons and found
pyjamas. He was shivering.

'I'll make you a hot-water bottle,' I said.

In the kitchen I had the tap running to fill the kettle but
there was a noise from the bedroom. I turned off the tap.
A terrible kind of moan. I dropped the kettle in the sink
and ran the length of the corridor. I thought heart attack.

'What's the matter?' I called out as I ran. My voice was
on the way to a scream. 'What is it? What's wrong?'

His teeth were chattering. He did not look at me but
lay with eyes half closed beneath the trembling bedclothes.

'It's OK,' he said. 'I think I've got a chill.'

'Why did you make that noise?' I asked.

It's only my m-m-my teeth chattering,' he said through
a new wave. 'Bb bw I'mmb fr-fr-freezing.' He sucked in
breath through his trembling jaw.

Clive's pale face floated on the dark-brown bed linen
against dark brown carpet. I took his temperature. It was
above normal.

'I'm calling the doctor.'

'No need,' he said. 'I'm probably fighting off
something.'

He was the husband. I was used to taking his word
for it.

I believe that shuddering was the first slight jar to Clive's brain, perhaps a momentary seizure.

Our cousin Lawrence felt only a slight jar one night on a voyage to America. He went on deck and spoke with people playing cards. They'd felt it too but went on shuffling. Our cousin never saw them again. They were on the *Titanic*. Lawrence got out alive in a half-full lifeboat as so many women refused to leave their husbands, preferring to drown with them than to survive widowed. 'In some cases,' said our cousin, 'they were torn from their husbands and pushed into the boats, but in many instances they were allowed to remain, since there was no-one to insist.'

Wearing's memoir, *Forever Today*, tells the story of the illness which struck down her husband, a gifted conductor and music producer, leaving him with a total amnesia, trapped in the constantly recurring moment. This passage from near the beginning creates a strong narrative tension as almost everything that happens, from the sudden storm to Clive's comment, 'I can't cope with a film or anything with a plot,' resonates with ominous feeling. Even the expression 'That day' in the first line creates a narrative pull. Read this memoir for its absorbing story of a love that endures despite the loss of a remembered self.

WRITING EXERCISES

1. A day in the life

Select a recent day in your life, within the last couple of weeks, and simply recount what happened that day. Do not plan it; simply write what you can remember. See whether it has a narrative. If you can see narrative elements, start cutting away what is not necessary and perhaps writing in more detail whatever seems significant. *(20 minutes)*

2. Scenes

Write ten separate short pieces from a period or a relationship in your life, taking no more than half a page for each one. Do the exercise over a few days if you need to. Write the scenes in any order, just as you think of them, but note which one you wrote first, second, etc. Then sort them into what you think is the best order for the unfolding of the narrative. See how close that is to the order in which you wrote them. *(15 minutes for each piece)*

3. Plotting forwards and backwards

Select an event that has unfolded in your life, one where you can see a beginning, a middle and a conclusion. Write it in three paragraphs, one for each section, first of all in that order. Then try it beginning at the end and telling it backwards. This does not mean simply shuffling the paragraphs but writing them again, so that the story works told backwards. A number of films have used this technique, starting at the end of a relationship and then showing scenes progressively back in time to the beginning. It can be a very poignant way of plotting a story. See whether forwards or backwards works best for your story. *(1 hour)*

4. Once upon a time

Begin a story from your life with the words 'Once upon a time' and continue to unfold the story, but use fairytale vocabulary only. If someone helped you, they were a 'wise woman' who gave you an 'amulet'. If you had difficult times, you were 'lost in a swamp' or 'traversing dark caves under the mountains' or 'lost in the dark wood'. The key to this exercise is the use of symbolic language and the translation of events in your life into mythic events. Do not use modern jargon, nor personal names, nor precise historical occurrences. Write it briefly, no more than three pages. See whether it has revealed the bones of the story you want to write. *(30 minutes)*

8.
TRUE CONFESSIONS
— TRUTH-TELLING

TRUTH, JOHN KEATS said, is a beautiful thing. 'Truth is Beauty; Beauty, Truth.' The words, so familiar, even commonplace, are thrilling every time they are fully considered. The idea that truth, by its nature, is beautiful and that beauty, by its nature, is truthful, is an irresistible one for any writer, any artist. It is poetic insight of the highest order, economical and encompassing at once. Perhaps it is 'all ye know on earth and all ye need to know'. But for the memoirist, truth is rarely so beautifully poetic, especially in the beginning. It is complex, messy, confronting and fraught with dangers.

For a start, there are many reasons not to tell the truth. As another English poet, John Donne, said, 'No man is an island.' No woman either. You are part of a family, a circle of friends, a social or professional community, a country. All of these groups have varying levels of tolerance for the truth, and, without it being stated, you know the rules. You know not to tell your mother about your father's affair because it would break her heart. You know to talk only about the happy side of life to a work colleague because that is all she wants to hear. You know that stating a particular political viewpoint will alienate half your school community. You know not to tell the truth every time you open your mouth. You and everyone else. In daily life, most people who are not sociopaths edit the things they say. It can be a difficult habit to break when you come to the page.

Not that it is simply a habit. It would be much easier if it were. Editing the self comes not just from a sense of what is appropriate, from obeying social rules, but also from a desire not to cause pain. If you write about the impact of being aware of your father's affair when you were a teenager but not telling your mother, what is that going to do to your mother now? What will it do to your favourite aunt if you write about your uncle molesting you? What will your children feel if you write that you had never wanted to get married and have babies? The likelihood of hurting or up-setting family members is the strongest single argument against telling the truth.

Sometimes, with family and neighbours, it is not as serious as avoiding hurt, but simply the desire to avoid embarrassing someone, or a wish not to invade their privacy. There are many things hidden within families and many confidences given. Do you have the right to reveal information given to you in confidence, or even things you observed that may now be embarrassing to others? Do you have the right to tell the world your mother was an alcoholic, knowing it will mortify your very proper sister? What about revealing that the boy next door liked to wear girls' nighties when he was little, knowing that he is now a federal politician? How far is too far?

In the wider community — in your work, school, sports group or church — there are practical reasons for not telling the truth. If people in your small country town knew you were gay, would they still attend your medical practice? If your church community knew you had a baby when you were fifteen, would they still treat you the same? It is not that you are hurting others in such revelations, but you may be affecting the way others respond to you.

There may also be legal and personal safety considerations putting pressure on telling the truth. One woman writing a memoir about a long mental illness was concerned that a particular doctor could sue her if she revealed what she considered his misdiagnosis. Another woman writing about her involvement with the African National Congress in the 1970s in South Africa was concerned her revelations about men who were now in power might endanger her or her children. A man writing about his clandestine missionary activity in China was worried he might be endangering the lives of the Chinese people who had helped him.

Sometimes the pressure is simply that you want to be 'nice'. Women especially feel the pressure to smooth things over, to keep the peace, to make everyone feel comfortable. Virginia Woolf personified this pressure as 'the Angel in the House' who was *so constituted that she never had a mind or a wish of her own, but preferred always to sympathise with the minds and wishes of other.* For many women writing a memoir, this can be the least conscious but strongest pressure against truth-telling.

How can the truth be told when there are so many valid reasons not to? And do you always need to tell the truth anyway?

Truth-telling — some non-literary considerations

- Check your motives. I don't mean literary motivations, such as whether the structure needs it, but personal motives. All memoirists probably have non-literary motives for some of the things they write — for example, to honour someone, to criticise someone, to give thanks. The writer is not exempt from responsibility to others, however, and some motives are clearly more just than others. What is the reason for revealing this piece of dirty underwear? If the story and themes concern dirty under-wear, then by all means reveal it, but if the reason is to embarrass or inflict pain, then its inclusion might be reconsidered. The truth, the whole truth, is important and no one can go forward without it, but as American memoirist Annie Dillard said, 'Writing is an art, not a martial art.'

- If the truth you have to tell will hurt others, weigh up its importance. This includes its emotional importance to you and its narrative or thematic importance. Does your story need the revelation about Aunt Kate's much younger lover? Perhaps yes, if it shaped your own sense of sexuality, and perhaps yes, if it affected the family dynamic. There is no absolute answer, but if it is necessary to your purpose, include it; if not, weigh up whether your story can do without it.

- If you have decided the truth you want to write is important, consider how many people it will damage, and how severely. Include yourself in this tally. This is not to say that you should avoid the truth if the numbers are too high and the disruption too great, it is simply to say: be aware of it. You can decide whether you are prepared to weather the storm. Although truth, however subjective, is central to memoir, each writer needs to weigh up for himself if he is ready for emotional storms that could damage relationships with family and friends.

- Consider the unreliability of memory. Although memory is fascinating, complex and often the only truth we have, it is manifestly not a totally reliable witness. All of us are made of our memories, they constitute the fabric of ourselves, and it feels like a betrayal of self to question memory. But while a memory always has value, it is clear that not all memories are equally valid. At least allow room for other possibilities.

It may sound as if the truth is impossible; I mean only to acknowledge the difficulty. There is no point in dodging the taboos against the truth because they can prevent you from going forward with your writing. Facing them, you can continue. There are a few ways to tell the truth and survive.

Writing the truth

- The tone of voice you use will make a great deal of difference to how your truths are received. *It's not what she said; it's how she said it.* If your tone of voice is whining, accusing or bitter, then most people will find your words unpalatable, no matter how true. It is a curious fact that bitterness and self-pity, in particular, are universally un- appealing — both imply that everything is someone else's fault. If your tone of voice is clear and direct, then even unpleasant truths can be listened to. Of course, all this depends on your own relationship to the truth. If you still feel bitter about something, it's not worth faking a relaxed tone of voice — it is rarely convincing. It might be best to try and work it out in the first draft.
- Say everything you want to say in the first draft — you can take it out later. If a particularly distressing episode feels too exposing to write — drunken father turning up at school and abusing your favourite teacher — tell your- self it is secret writing, that it is only for your eyes. If you

want to scream and rant about something, even if you want to preach about something, do it in the first draft. It might mean that you go places you would otherwise not have gone; it might also mean that you realise it does not look so bad written down.

- Remind yourself that writing is not about being 'nice'. The truth would never be told if everyone kept up a smooth and smiling front. Sometimes, the Angel in the House has to be locked in the wardrobe, at least during the first draft. Truth has more power than 'nice'. (Although 'nice' in its rarely used sense of 'most precise' can be very powerful.)

- Remember that 'the truth' is not just about painful or unpleasant events. It can be just as difficult, sometimes even more difficult, to be truthful about happiness because, very often, happiness is not well observed. Even though it was Tolstoy who said it, I don't agree that 'all happy families are happy in the same way'. It is more that the details of happiness are not noted with the same attention as the details of pain. Try to write the details of happiness, of love and parental pride and delight, with attention to the particulars.

- Telling the truth, especially when it involves what has happened to other people in your life, can be a matter of finding your perspective, your relationship to the story. What happens to other people is not necessarily your business, but sometimes it is. What happened to your sister in Africa may be part of your story if it reveals a key aspect of your relationship to her. Find out what matters to you about the story and you will find your perspective and how to tell it.

- Consider the saving grace of humour. Many difficult topics can be written about — and read — more easily if

there is a humorous or ironic approach. It doesn't mean
that you should be flippant about serious topics, but even
the heaviest subject can have a humorous aspect. In
Running with Scissors, Augusten Burroughs writes about
his mother's avid and destructive desire for fame with
such humour that the reader can see the truth but does
not have to feel judgmental:

Okay, now I need your honest reaction. Did it feel
powerful to you? Emotionally charged?' I knew the only
correct answer to this question was, 'Wow. That really does
seem like something you'd read in the *New Yorker.*' She
laughed, pleased. 'Really? Do you really think so? The *New
Yorker* is very selective. They don't publish just anyone.

- Admitting to your readers that your memoir is your
version of events, your perspective, can be disarming.
There are nearly always contending versions of events in
any life, the more so when there is conflict, and admitting
to this reality means that at least family and friends have
some room to move. Being absolute is often irritating.
Uncertainty is often more appealing and more believable
than adamant assertion that will not hear of any other
possibility.
- Talk to the people concerned if possible. It may not be
possible, lack of communication may be part of the problem but sometimes, especially if people are given the
chance to air their point of view, it can make it easier for
you to write yours. Susan Varga says that she showed an
early draft of her memoir, *Heddy and Me*, to her mother,
who was upset at first by her daughter's view of her. Varga
showed her the manuscript again at proof stage and her
mother was still bothered, but more fascinated by the
process of a life becoming a story. When the book was

published, her mother read it again and by now was thrilled to be the subject of a book. I am not saying everyone will be thrilled to be in your memoir, but people do change their responses. It can be worth persisting.

- Be aware of the difference between fact and truth. Any number of facts do not necessarily add up to truth; facts are true, but to contain truth they must convey some illumination, some insight. A manuscript I read recently contained endless facts about religious life, but it did not reveal to me any truthful insight about such a life. It is usually dull to include lots of facts about dates, times, places, and people that do not convey anything other than an accurate record.

- On the other hand, it is a good idea to check the facts, particularly information that is a matter of record. It can be embarrassing to get the facts wrong — I still squirm when I see the wrongly named church in one of my earlier books. More seriously, in some circumstances you could even be sued. However, if it is necessary to include a lot of factual material in your memoir, it is a good idea not to spend too much time on research — it is often very difficult to begin writing when you have spent a lot of time and energy on research. I find it better to write and leave gaps — to check the facts afterwards.

- Consider changing identifying details. This is generally not the best course of action as the people who know you will still be able to identify characters, and for the general reader it does not matter anyway; but if there is a risk of legal action, or of identifying someone who does not want to be identified for a good reason, then it might be worth changing details such as place names, dates, people's names — if these details are not crucial to the story. In *Whatever The Gods Do* I changed the names of everyone because the child I was writing about was, by then, a teenager, and I did not want him to be embarrassed at school. I did not change any of the details of events or actions, as these were the essential facts of the story.

- Writing your memoir 'as a novel' to avoid the difficulty of exposing truth is often suggested but, as I have said, this is generally not a good idea. The memoir and the novel require allegiance to different kinds of truth; one to the truth of what actually happened, the other to the integrity of its structure. (See chapter 2 for further discussion of this topic.)

Too much information

There's a phrase teenagers use if an adult tells them anything they find embarrassing — 'too much information'. *Stop right now, however much you want to tell me, I do not need to know these details.* Trying to construct your perception of truth on the page can feel like walking a narrow line between 'too much information' and skimming the surface. Memoir, by its nature, can easily tip over into details which, rather than enlightening the reader, make them squirm. These can be details about bodily functions, including sex, but can also be what feels like invasive information about parents, lovers or friends. The reader feels that the memoirist has gone too far.

On the other hand, it can be just as easy to avoid the truth by omission, by simply leaving out whatever feels too difficult. The reader is left sensing the gaps and feeling cheated that she has not been trusted with the truth. How far is too far? How to walk that line between too much and too little? For a start, maybe you want to make your reader squirm. That, I suppose, is a legitimate aim. If that is what you are interested in, why not push the boundaries of comfort?

Many memoirists at present are declaring the end of boundaries so that the reader can enjoy burping, urinating,
scratching — all completely human activities, of course. If
you want to include such details, it really is a matter of your
intention, the effect that you want your memoir to have.
If it is to impress upon the reader the banal physicality of life,
for instance, or the absurd and comic nature of pretensions,
then this is a necessary part of your material. The breaking
of taboos has its place in memoir, but the more shocking the
material, the more crucial the voice you use to convey it.
Personally, I enjoy a contrast between tone and material, such
as the contrast between the calm, correct voice and the
startling sexual material of *The Sexual Life of Catherine M* by
Catherine Millet.

It becomes problematic when 'going too far' is in
emotional or psychological territory, especially when it
involves, as it must, other people's lives. Many times in class,
students express their outrage that a writer has gone too far
in exposing a mother's faults or a lover's inner thoughts.
Outraging a sense of privacy can be more shocking than
outraging a sense of propriety, but again, there are no hard-
and-fast rules, for each person has a different sense of what is
private. I can only say, follow your own sense of privacy,
expose what you feel needs to be exposed, keep hidden what
is not necessary for readers to know.

A sense of privacy should not, however, be used as an
excuse for sweeping everything unpleasant under the carpet,
or as an excuse not to trust the reader with difficult material.
There is nothing so unnourishing, or unbelievable, as a
memoir which gives only the light and sweetness of life. It is
like eating fairy floss — pretty and fun to eat at a carnival,
but unsatisfying and boring for a long-term diet. Sometimes
you might have to push your sense of privacy — peek into

the tent and see how the fairy floss is manufactured — the oily machinery and sweaty arms. Sometimes you have to give yourself a push into the taboo territory.

That's not to say that everything ought to be exposed in great detail. Going into too much detail can become self-indulgent (see chapter 9). What is not said can be as powerful, sometimes even more powerful, than what is said: withholding the full horror lets it expand in the reader's mind, rather than it being constrained by your words. In Skye Rogers' *Drink Me*, she is restrained about the mother of her boyfriend, only letting the reader see that she sweeps compulsively, day and night. The reader is left to conjecture what this might mean. Rogers respects the privacy of his family while giving the reader a useful glimpse. This kind of brief image — words that suggest more than they say — can be very effective when you do not want to expose others to scrutiny but still want to tell the truth.

Truth and glitter

A photograph can make the most banal of scenes look 'interesting' or 'romantic'. The stilling of the flux of life, the choice of light and the framing, give the illusion of complete-ness, an ordinary life made into art. It is just as easy to over-polish experience with words and make it so 'shiny' that it no longer bears much relationship to raw reality. Truth is a slippery creature and it can just as well hide itself in pleasing language as in avoidance or self-indulgence. The more experienced and skilled you become as a writer, the more temptation there is to give everything the frame and gloss of a photograph. 'I seal loose ends with cadenced prose and add glitter where I know things were quite lustreless,' comments American writer Andre Aciman in his essay, 'Lies Sweet Lies'.

It is not to say that this is necessarily a bad thing — beauty is truth, after all. But perhaps beauty can be emptied of truth. Perhaps it can happen that when beauty is the aim, truth can be lost and beauty becomes over-elegant and formal. Sometimes what is required, as an earlier American writer, Henry Miller, said, is 'a gob of spit in the face of Art'. There is a raw energy, a fierceness of experience, which can be lost when you focus entirely on the words. Then you may need to write with your heart and with your gut, pegging the bloody mess out on the page without concern for appearance. Write wildly, fiercely, unrestrainedly, disturbingly, passionately. Write without respect, write inappropriately, scream if you want to. Write with only the fierce discipline of the desire for truth to guide you.

In any case, it is always difficult to know the truth, especially about yourself. Each one of us has a preferred version of ourselves and even in our secret moments we can entertain that version quite satisfactorily. We can maintain it for years too; Chilean writer Isabel Allende wrote a story, *Tosca*, about a woman who managed to maintain an illusion for her whole life about the 'Great Love' for which she had abandoned her loving husband and child. Even when the facts contradicted her, she held onto the myth of her life. Such a feat is not uncommon. There are doubts about the adequacy of the self, which we can cunningly hide even from our own conscious awareness. Perhaps all writers write to build a screen against that doubt. As Andre Aciman says, 'We write about our life, not to see it as it was, but to see it as we wish others might see it, so we may borrow their gaze …'

Still, the truth, however one imagines it, seems to me to be something worth trying for. Despite the quicksands of 'too much information' and the glossy shine of the stylish facade, there is a way through which is yours alone. There is

the possibility of putting down on the page what I in-
adequately term 'a real relationship with what is'. Where does
this possibility lie? It comes when you let go the desire to impress, the greatest pollutant of the truth. The desire to impress
others with our cleverness, sensitiveness, awareness, insight,
begins by muddying and ends up supplanting the desire for
truth. If you can write free of that desire, then you have a
good chance of writing clear, passionate truth. You will recognise it when you have, even if you have never seen it before.
It will have a beauty that is unmistakable.

READING

Running with Scissors

by Augusten Burroughs

She stood up from the sofa and walked slowly across the
white shag carpeting, as if finding her mark on a sound
stage. 'I'm hysterical?' she asked in a smooth, low voice.
'You think *this* is hysterical?' She laughed theatrically,
throwing her head back. 'Oh, you poor bastard. You lousy
excuse for a man.' She stood next to him, leaning her back
against the teak bookcase. 'You're so repressed you mistake
creative passion for hysterics. And don't you see? This is
how you are killing me.' She closed her eyes and made her
Edith Piaf face.

My father moved away from her. He brought the glass
to his lips and took a deep swallow from his drink.
Because he'd been drinking all evening, his words were
slightly blurry. 'Nobody's trying to kill you, Deirdre. You're
killing yourself.'

'I wish you'd rot in hell,' she spat. 'I regret the day I
ever married you.'

While they were fighting, I was sitting at the dining-room table fastening and unfastening the lobster claw clasp on the gold chain my mother had bought me in Amherst. I worried constantly that it would fall from my neck. And the only thing that reassured me was to test its dependability over and over again. I glanced up and said, 'Can't you two *stop* fighting. You always fight and I hate it.'

'This is between me and your father,' my mother said coldly.

'No it's not,' I shouted with surprising volume. 'It's not just between you because I'm here too. And I can't stand it. All you ever do is scream at each other. Can't you just leave each other alone? Can't you try?'

My mother replied, 'Your father is the one who is making things difficult for us.'

Eventually the fight moved next door to the kitchen, providing them with better lighting as well as potential weapons.

'Look at your damn face,' my mother said. 'You've got the face of a man twice your age. Thirty-seven years old going on' eighty.'

My father was very drunk by now and the only way he could imagine restoring silence to the house was to stop my mother from breathing.

'Get your damn hands *off* me,' my mother screamed, struggling against my father's hands, which had found their way around her neck.

'Shut the hell up, you bitch.' His teeth were clenched.

I had followed them into the kitchen, and was standing in the doorway in my Snoopy pyjamas. 'Stop!' I screamed. 'Stop this!'

In one motion, my mother shoved my drunk father, sending him reeling backward against the kitchen counter.

His head hit the dishwasher on the way down and when he made contact with the kitchen floor, he didn't move. A small pool of blood began to form under his ear and I was sure he was dead.

'He's not moving,' I said, moving closer.

'The spineless bastard is only playing another one of his pitiful games.' She nudged his bad knee with her red toe. 'Get up, Norman. You're frightening Augusten. Enough of your pranks.'

My father eventually sat up, leaning his head against the dishwasher.

With disgust, my mother tore a Bounty paper towel from the roll and handed it to him. 'I should just let you bleed to death for terrifying our son like that.'

He pressed it against the side of his face to absorb the blood.

Seeing that my father was still alive, I was now worried about my mother. '*Please* don't hurt her,' I said. '*Please* don't kill her.' The problem was that my father's unemotional nature scared me. There was a difference between the calm expression of the man on a jar of Taster's Choice coffee and the blank expression my father wore. I was afraid he was, like my mother said, bottled with rage, ready to snap.

Again, I leaned forward. *'Please don't kill her.'*

'Your father isn't going to kill me,' my mother said, switching on the front burner of the stove, pulling a More from her pack, and leaning over to light it on the heating coil. 'He'd rather suffocate me with his horribly oppressive manipulation and then wait for me to cut my own throat.'

'Will you please just shut the hell up, Deirdre?' my father said, weary and drunk.

My mother smiled down at him, blowing smoke

through her nostrils. 'I will *please shut the hell up* the day you *please drop the hell dead.*'

I was seized with panic. 'Are you going to cut your own throat?' I asked her.

She smiled and held out her arms. 'No, of course not. That's just a figure of speech.' She kissed the top of my head and scratched my back. 'Now, it's nearly one in the morning; way past your bedtime. You need to go to sleep so you can be ready for school in the morning.'

I walked off to my room where I selected an outfit for school and carefully arranged it on hangers at the front of the closet. I would wear my favourite polyester tan pants and a blue shirt with the vest cleverly sewn on. If only I had a pair of platform shoes the outfit would be complete.

Still, knowing my clothes were ready gave me a sense of calm. I could *control* the sharpness of the crease in my double-knit slacks, even if I couldn't stop my mother from hurling the Christmas tree off the porch like she did one winter. I could polish my 14k gold-plated signet ring with a Q-tip until the gold-plating wore off even if I couldn't stop my parents from throwing John Updike novels at each other's heads.

So I became consumed with making sure my jewelry was just as reflective as Donnie Osmond's and my hair was perfectly smooth, like plastic.

In *Running with Scissors*, Burroughs pulls out all stops as he re-creates the instability first of his parents, then the even more insane household of his mother's psychiatrist where he spent his adolescent years. He writes with sometimes unpalatable or harrowing detail, but holds his readers every moment with his humour. He goes to the heart of the monsters in his childhood, observes everything, right down to the brand names, and examines himself with the same truthful, sardonic eye. Read this memoir for its searing and comic truthfulness.

WRITING EXERCISES

1. Secret writing

Simply write about yourself, some incident, something you have done or thought which does not incriminate anyone else, but you prefer no one knew about. Write with the full knowledge that no one is ever going to see it. It is not going to be part of your memoir. Notice the freedom you feel knowing there will be no judgment of the incident, no evaluation of the writing. You can even destroy it when you are done. But before you do, read it through. See if there is anything in it worth salvaging. *(20 minutes)*

2. Opening the closet

Write an episode that you know someone you care about would not like you to write. It may involve them or just you. Again, remind yourself that no one need see this piece of writing. When you are finished, clarify whether you want to include the incident in a memoir, and why or why not. *(20 minutes)*

3. Breaking taboos

Write about a topic that makes you squirm. It can be anything from bodily functions to embarrassing flaws. Write it twice, once from a serious or, if you like, impartial perspective, once from a humorous perspective. Try being ironic, try exaggerating. *(10 minutes each)*

4. Happy days

Write about an experience that carries strong positive emotions — anything from parental pride to love to happiness. This might sound like an easy exercise, but generally it is even more difficult to write about happy times because, very often, they are less well observed than unhappiness. Try to avoid generalities, instead noting precise details of the experience. *(20 minutes)*

9.
THE BIG 'I' — SELF-INDULGENCE AND CONTEXT

YEARS AGO AT university, I used to present a radio program which had a literary arts segment. Writers submitted their work and I and a colleague read through the manuscripts and selected extracts, which we then presented live to air. The radio station was at the top of a skyscraper and we enjoyed the feeling of raining the poems and stories gently down on the city below. One day we arrived late and did not have time to read a set of poems before going to air. When the time for the arts segment came, I picked up the sheaf of poems and began reading. It wasn't long before I wished we had arrived on time.

The cool air of the studio felt turgid, muddied. It was as if I were tipping a vial of infectious ooze into the microphone and wilfully letting it drip down over the broadcast audience. I could almost see it pouring down from the telecommunications tower, spreading out over the buildings and streets and parks of the city. The poems were the wounded outpourings of personal anguish, written with the self-absorption of a sufferer who could not see beyond her own world. She had tried to write truthfully from within her pain and illness but had not taken the necessary step of transforming it with the art of language into intense and moving poetry. What she offered was still 'runny', 'sticky', unformed.

Her subject was not the problem. The American poet Sylvia Plath wrote with fierce, powerful energy and searing honesty about the same territory of inner pain, her suffering forged into steely, beautifully formed poetry. This author was drowning in a swamp of suffering and self-pity — and trying to drag the reader and listeners in with her.

Poetry is not the only art in which there is a danger of self-indulgence. Every few months, in the arts section of newspapers, or sometimes in a stray column, there is a journalistic outburst condemning the self-indulgence of memoir. And, on occasion, when I mention my passion for memoir, a shadow of judgment creeps into the eyes of the listener. I recognise the shadow because every memoirist fears the judgment that memoir and autobiography is an excuse for undisciplined self-indulgence, that memoirists are navel-gazers of the highest order, that they use the excuse of truth for pouring their self-absorption out onto the page. Why would anyone want to read it? What makes you think anyone is interested in your particular angst?

People do often ask me, 'Isn't autobiographical writing egotistical and self-indulgent?' In my experience it is most often the opposite — in fact, one of the most striking aspects of life writing classes is that the struggle to make sense of being here on this planet creates not self-absorption, but a rare warmth, a bond. Writing and sharing one's story breaks down the feeling of a disconnected, superior self and builds a sense of a community of being human in a puzzling world. Understanding our own experience connects us more deeply to others; offering it to others creates a community of understanding. I would even go so far as to say that really hearing each other's stories unties knots of conflict and creates compassion. Writing about the self is one of the most demanding journeys you can take. It requires honesty, ruthlessness and courage. At the same time, the pitfalls of self-indulgence are real.

What, exactly, is self-indulgence? There is often a faint note of defensiveness in the question. Everyone has a different sensibility about it, but for me, memoir becomes self-indulgent when the author falls in on her subject, forgetting the reader and forgetting language. Avoiding self-indulgence is not about avoiding certain subjects — you can write about anything you want, no topic is taboo — but it is about remembering that you are creating a world made out of words for a reader to inhabit.

To avoid self-indulgence, first face that original accusing question, 'Why would anyone want to read it?' It is not so difficult to find the answer. Ask yourself, 'Why do I want to write it?' If the answer is simply to empty the bucket full of rubbish you have inside you, then very possibly your memoir is for yourself alone, not for a reader. If you feel there is something of value in the rubbish, make your first draft a bucket-emptying procedure, then get to work on it, creating something for your reader to use.

It requires taking that one step back from the subject to become the narrator, still close enough to feel it, but not so close that you are drowning in a swamp of self-absorption. The 'I' who is telling the story steps back from being the protagonist to being the narrator. This often requires the simple solution of time. If you are too close to the experience in time, then it is often difficult to take the necessary step back. Wait a bit longer. But it is also an inner step back from the material, looking at it in a ruthless way as material rather than as your life. In some sense, writers must be scavengers — picking through the bits and pieces and selecting what they want.

It also requires you to remember that you are writing this for someone to read. It means you are communicating rather than throwing up. It means you are aware that you are not simply pouring yourself out; you are making something out of words. You remind yourself that *my stomach was knotted in despair* might not be the most original way of conveying your feelings. You remember the transforming power of fresh, evocative language.

It is possible to tell the whole truth with intensity and power, but experience and words are not the same thing. Each shapes the other; we form words and words form us. As writers, we must align ourselves with words, trying to create simulacra or representations of experience.

A wider world

Even when you have avoided the swamp of self-indulgence, it can feel as if the world you have created on the page is too self-centred. It can be horrifying to look back on what you have written and see a forest of 'I's. It's not to say that the 'I' is always self-centred; a memoir must be written from the first person, and this personal perspective, this access to the inner life, is part of what makes it so appealing. But at times it can revolve too tightly around the 'I', creating a claustrophobic, suffocating atmosphere. The reader feels as if they are being dragged into a vortex of self, rather than taken on a journey of exploration of the self.

It is possible to remove some of the self-centredness, some of the forest of 'I's, by simply writing from an impersonal perspective. Instead of writing 'I' each time as you name your response to your environment, evoke the event, scene or person in such a way that the reader can see your response. For example: *I loved the pear tree flowering outside my window* could be rewritten: *There was an elegant pear tree with creamy blossoms outside my window.* The reader does not always need to be told, but instead can be led to see with your eyes, respond with your sensibility, without 'I' directing everything.

The self-indulgence may not just be the overuse of 'I'. It could well be that, because you are concentrating on following a particular narrative, you have made a world that is too small, too centred on the self. It can leave no room for the reader to stand. Whatever the experience you are writing about, readers need a place to position themselves in relation to it. Otherwise it is like coming into a conversation halfway through — without a context it is difficult to know what is going on and therefore how to relate to the information. You might hear *Mrs van Gelder killed her husband* — but you don't know if Mrs van Gelder is a real-life neighbour, or a character in a soap opera, so you don't know how to interpret this, or how to respond.

In memoir, especially if your experience is outside the mainstream, readers will need a context so that they can find a way of relating to your experience. It simply means in-cluding enough experiences that most people will recognise — if you grew up in a closed religious sect, for example, details about meals, schooling and clothes will help readers recognise the difference of your life in relation to these ordinary aspects of their lives.

Much of the experience of life happens on an inner level. Thoughts, insights and meditations are all part of life but can have little or no connection with action or scenery. Trying to convey inner life can result in highly abstract, dense, self-centred writing, inaccessible to the reader. To open out that inner world, it can help to think like a film-maker. In films, characters rarely say everything they are thinking — unless it is a Woody Allen film — but their thoughts and feelings are revealed by the environments they inhabit and by their responses to the world around them. Writing about the world around you is a way of revealing yourself without self-absorption.

You can know what someone is like by what impresses him or her. This doesn't only mean that you can know what people are like according to whether they are impressed by money or wisdom, power or literary talent, it also means you can see what people are like according to what they notice — by what *impresses itself* upon their consciousness. Each person sees the world in a different way, notices different things, according to individual personalities and interests. One will notice the space, light and colour of a room, another the clothes of the people in the room, another the mood of particular people, another the expensive furniture. Each observation tells us something about the observer. If you write the details of your room, house, street, neighbourhood, the reader can see something of the person you are without you having to talk directly about yourself all the time.

There are also the wider worlds of history, politics, current affairs and science — in fact, all the worlds which make up your individual experience. It can be interesting to add research material that is wider than your personal knowledge. The areas you expand into will depend on your own interests and the scope of your memoir. Include a history of the Irish uprising of 1916 if your family was involved and your memoir explores your own commitment to causes. If you are writing a memoir about the women in your family, you could include the history and influence of feminism. If you are writing about the impact of an illness, include the science of the illness and its treatment. In *Pilgrim at Tinker Creek*, Annie Dillard includes considerable ecological knowledge as well as her own observations. A wider context, but one which is related to your specific memoir, will take the limelight away from you for a while and make it richer, more textured, more layered.

In *Whatever The Gods Do*, which partly told the story of a friend who suffered a cerebral haemorrhage and remained alive in a 'locked in' state for over a year, I included material about the nature of the brain and, in particular, what happens during a haemorrhage. I even included a diagram. Because her brain had been severely damaged by the haemorrhage it seemed necessary to me to include a scientific understanding of what had happened. But more than that, I've always been interested in the way we have so many ways of 'knowing' a situation, so many stories, from the emotional story of a friend to the scientific story of a doctor. These stories all come from different angles, from different bodies of knowledge, but they are all 'true', all necessary to the overall story of what has happened.

If you are interested in including research material, you will need to think about how to weave it into the rest of the text. You can put short extracts in whole, or you can rewrite in your own style. Short extracts work better if you are using a 'collage' approach where you are connecting many different short pieces. Generally speaking, too many extracts from other sources, too much undigested material, starts looking like you do not have confidence in your own material. Still, the approach of weaving other texts and other sources of information into your story to create a multi-layered effect can be very appealing and can offer a richer reading experience.

There are a number of issues to consider in looking

outwards in your memoir. If you go too far, you can end up writing a memoir in which you are absent. In class, an older man wrote comprehensively about his boyhood, including precise details about the dimensions and design of various rooms in the migrant hostel he lived in for several months, but there was little sense of how he felt in this new and alien environment. He was missing from his own memoir. It is much less threatening to write about the wider world, and taken to an extreme, it can become a social history rather than a memoir. Remember, a reader of a memoir essentially wants to know what it is like to be you.

There can also be the danger of adding layers that are not intrinsically related to the themes or narratives of the memoir. Very often I have seen manuscripts which include all sorts of extraneous history, science and current affairs, making it look as if the writer doesn't have enough material and is plumping it out with researched information. A detailed history of the battle between the Stuarts and McDonalds in Scotland might be interesting of itself, but it probably does not need to be in your story of a year on a sailing boat — even if you are of Scottish descent. It might be more relevant to find interesting material on oceanography or weather patterns, for example.

Adding too much material from a wider context can also result in a lumpy structure. One writer had been (badly) advised to write a 'big soup of a book', which resulted in the inclusion of a huge variety of things — including such information as the details of her research project on linguistics at university. This would have been fine if the memoir was shaped around the possibilities of language, but there was so much other material of every kind that it was impossible to discern what the memoir was about. It was a 'soup' with unrelated 'chunks' floating around in it, and the 'broth' wasn't strong enough to hold it together!

You need to be sensitive to the effect on the structure that additional material will have. An eclectic approach can work; you can include a wide range of outward-looking information, especially if you have a roving mind interested in all sorts of things, but you need to be aware of the effect on the shape of your memoir. A memoir is about you, that is true, but it is more accurately about an experience of being. According to the extent and shape of the memoir, it will include elements of your physical, social, political, scientific and other environments as they influence and even determine your experience of being. The 'I' will be there, letting the reader see what it is like inside and outside the millimetres of skin separating us from each other.

READING

The Year of Magical Thinking
                                        by Joan Didion

In time of trouble, I had been trained since childhood, read, learn, work it up, go to the literature. Information was control. Given that grief remained the most general of afflictions its literature seemed remarkably spare. There was the journal C.S. Lewis kept after the death of his wife, *A Grief Observed*. There was the occasional passage in one or another novel, for example Thomas Mann's description in *The Magic Mountain* of the effect on Hermann Castorp of his wife's death: 'His spirit was troubled; he shrank within himself; his benumbed brain made him blunder in his business so that the firm of Castorp and Son suffered sensible financial losses; and the next spring while inspecting his warehouses on the windy landing-stage, he got inflammation of the lungs. The fever was too much for his shaken heart, and in five days, notwithstanding all

Dr Heidekind's care, he died.' There were, in classical
ballets, the moments when one or another abandoned lover
tries to find and resurrect one or another loved one, the
blued light, the white tutus, the pas de deux with the loved
one that foreshadows the final return to the dead: *la danse
des ombres*, the dance of the shades. There were certain
poems, in fact, many poems. There was a day or two when
I relied on Matthew Arnold, 'The Forsaken Merman':

> *Children's voices should be dear*
> *(Call once more) to a mother's ear;*
> *Children's voices, wild with pain —*
> *Surely she will come again!*

There were days when I relied on W.H. Auden, the
'Funeral Blues' lines from *The Ascent of F6*:

> *Stop all the clocks, cut off the telephone,*
> *Prevent the dogs from barking with a juicy bone,*
> *Silence the pianos and with muffled drum*
> *Bring out the coffin, let the mourners come.*

The poems and the dances of the shades seemed the most
exact to me.

Beyond or below such abstracted representations of the
pains and furies of grieving, there was a body of sub-
literature, how-to guides for dealing with the condition,
some 'practical,' some 'inspirational,' most of either useless.
(Don't drink too much, don't spend the insurance money
redecorating the living room, join a support group.) That
left the professional literature, the studies done by the
psychiatrists and psychologists and social workers who

came after Freud and Melanie Klein, and quite soon it was
to this literature that I found myself turning. I learned
from it many things I already knew, which at a certain
point seemed to promise comfort, validation, an outside
opinion that I was not imagining what appeared to be
happening. From *Bereavement: Reactions, Consequences, and
Care*, compiled in 1984 by the National Academy of
Sciences' Institute of Medicine, I learned for example that
the most frequent responses to death were shock,
numbness and a sense of disbelief: 'Subjectively, survivors
may feel like they are wrapped in a cocoon or blanket; to
others, they may look as if they are holding up well.
Because the reality of death has not yet penetrated
awareness, survivors can appear to be quite accepting of
the loss.'

Here, then, we had the 'pretty cool customer' effect.

I read on. Dolphins, I learned from J. William Worden
of the Harvard Child Bereavement Study at Massachusetts
General Hospital, had been observed refusing to eat after
the death of a mate. Geese had been observed reacting to
such a death by flying and calling, searching until they
themselves became disoriented and lost. Human beings,
I read but did not need to learn, showed similar patterns of
response. They searched. They stopped eating. They forgot
to breathe. They grew faint from lowered oxygen, they
clogged their sinuses with unshed tears and ended up in
otolaryngologists' offices with obscure ear infections. They
lost concentration. 'After a year, I could read headlines,'
I was told by a friend whose husband had died three years
before. They lost cognitive ability on all scales. Like
Hermann Castorp they blundered in business and suffered
sensible financial losses. They forgot their own telephone
numbers and showed up at airports without picture ID.

They fell sick, they failed, they even, again like Hermann Castorp, died.

Didion's memoir exploring her grief at the death of her husband is an extraordinary example of how to write the most overwhelming experience with emotional intensity, but without a trace of self-indulgence. She attends to both the outer and inner details of her responses, she does not shy away from the painful reality, but because her purpose is to coax words into illuminating a fundamental human experience, the reader is not plunged into self-absorption but is inspired by the honesty and perceptiveness of her journey.

WRITING EXERCISES

1. Emptying the bucket

This exercise has two parts. First, write about an experience that carries strong negative emotion — anything from anger to shame to grief. Write it without restraint, without thought of how best to express it, without thought of anyone reading it. Then, a few days later, without reading your first piece, write about the same experience, but this time write it as if the piece has been commissioned for an anthology of memoir on this emotion. You are aware of trying to communicate the experience to strangers. *(20 minutes for each part)*

2. Avoiding indulgence

Write about someone who provokes strong emotions in you, whether positive or negative — love, pride, guilt, anger — but do not name the emotion anywhere in the piece. Begin with a particular physical mannerism, such as, 'He always cleared his throat before he spoke in company, a kind of muted fanfare so that he could be sure everyone was listening.' This is an exercise in avoiding self-indulgence and in disciplining your urge to spell everything out. You must observe and evoke a person without naming your responses to him or her. *(20 minutes)*

3. Research

Do some research related to your memoir. It can be from any area — science, music, medicine, politics, history — and then combine it with writing you have already done. Consider whether it works best woven seamlessly in, or placed as a separate piece, or perhaps broken into several shorter pieces. *(1 hour)*

4. Forest of 'I'

Write about a scene from any time of your life, preferably a scene that involves your perceptions of your environment. If you are stuck for a scene, perhaps evoke the first place you lived when you left home — the apartment or house, the people, an interaction with a house-mate. Leave it until the next day. Now try and write it again, this time cutting the number of 'I's in it by half by changing the perspective from which you are writing. *(30 minutes for each part of the exercise)*

10.
WISH YOU WERE HERE — TRAVEL WRITING

Dear Hope,

The coconut palms are swaying in the tropical breeze and in front of me the aqua sea looks like a dreamscape beneath the blue sky. The resort is set amongst hibiscus and frangipani — and every evening the friendly island people sing and dance for us. (In other words, I have the best life because I am here and this card is intended to make you envious. I am not going to mention the infected coral-scrape on my knee, or the motor-mouth woman in the next room who keeps bailing me up to go shopping with her, or the fact that Max looks so fat and white in his bathers that I do not want to sit with him at the pool.)
Wish you were here,

Verity

The postcard: the shortest, most common, and possibly the most dishonest form of travel writing!

Perhaps that's being too hard on all the innocent postcard writers who simply want to stay in touch with family and friends, but whenever I write a postcard, I am conscious of editing out all but the most 'glossy' experiences. It is as if there were a law forbidding the mention of anything that would disturb the smooth surface of happiness. Instead of clear truthfulness, a corny string of clichés on the back of a perfected image is posted across the world to end up on a mantelpiece or fridge.

It is easy to make the same mistake when you come to more extended travel writing. For me, travel or sojourn writing is essentially a branch of memoir — with all the same requirements of truth, clarity and evocative detail. Travel writing explores events, sights, people and experiences, just as memoir does — the defining difference being that the location is 'elsewhere' and that it is characteristically more outward looking than memoir. It is a wide genre and can include in-depth analysis of history, culture and politics, such as VS Naipaul's *India: A Wounded Civilisation*; it can emphasise characters and events, as John Berendt does in *Midnight in the Garden of Good and Evil*; or it can be a literary meditation on a city, such as Edmund White's *The Flâneur;* or a cross-over with philosophy such as Alain de Botton's *The Art of Travel*.

It is one of the most popular forms of memoir and it has its own pleasures and pitfalls, which deserve to be explored more closely. It is also worth looking at where travel writing came from, so first, a very brief, idiosyncratic history to give some idea of the depth and richness of travellers' tales.

Background

Travel writing appears to have existed in various forms at least as far back as *The Travels of Marco Polo*, which was written when he was in prison in Venice after his long journeys in the Orient in the thirteenth century. In a letter to a friend, the Italian poet Petrarch gave an account of his ascent of Mt Ventoux in 1336, one of the first pieces of literature expressing pleasure in travel for the sake of it. He remarked that his companions who did not want to climb the mountain showed 'a cold lack of curiosity'. Richard Hakluyt's *Voyages to the New World*, 1589, on the discovery of the Americas, is also considered a foundation text of travel writing.

But travel and travel writing didn't really develop a mass market until the nineteenth century when, in Europe, there was a great surge of interest in exotic lands. One of the most famous travellers was the English adventurer Richard Burton, who wrote numerous books about his journeys in dangerous and exotic lands, including *The Pilgrimage to Al Medina and Mecca*, 1855. A more gentle travel adventurer was Robert Louis Stevenson, who in 1879 wrote *Travels with a Donkey in the Cevennes*, the beginning of a long line of travel writing about the south of France. Nineteenth century women travellers were well represented by French traveller Flora Tristan's 1838 *Memoirs and Peregrinations of a Pariah*, and in 1910 Marie C Stopes' *A Journal from Japan*. Robert Byron's *The Road to Oxiana,* published in 1937, also belongs in this category of the learned and literary travel writer.

The twentieth century has seen a true explosion of travel writing as travel has come within the means of most westerners and many Asians. Some of the well-known names are Paul Theroux, Robyn Davidson, Jan Morris, Bruce Chatwin, Eric Newby and, more recently, Bill Bryson. Writers from countries colonised by Europe in the nineteenth century have also begun 'writing back'; for example, Caryl Phillips in *The European Tribe*.

These are just some of the names to look at if you are interested in becoming acquainted with and pursuing the art of travel and sojourn writing. To learn any genre of writing, it helps to read widely within it.

Where to go

As with any journey, the direction or aim of travel writing is the first consideration. Your purpose will determine, in many ways, the shape and style of your travel chronicles. Most short travel writing published in newspapers and magazines aims to promote a certain destination or activity and is not really part of travel memoir. It includes descriptions of place and atmosphere as well as information on sights, services and accommodation, and although it can be written from a personal perspective, it is about the place, not the traveller. It is travel journalism rather than travel memoir. A travel memoir often explores the traveller as much as it recounts the journey.

There are a number of main strands to travel memoir.

- *Adventure writing*: recounting exciting and/or romantic travellers' tales, as Thor Heyerdahl does in *Kon-Tiki*. There is a personal perspective, but the voice can be impersonal. The narrative of what happens is often more important than the traveller himself. The adventures can be physical (rafting down the Amazon River) or romantic (following someone you have only met once to a foreign country). It is narrative driven, meaning that the reader wants to find out what happens next. This obviously requires an adventurous spirit to try different and possibly dangerous travel experiences as well as the skill to create a strong narrative.

- *Character-based writing*: sketching or exploring individual people, and sometimes animals, in a foreign location, as in Gerald Durrell's *My Family and Other Animals*. The personal voice and perspective, often humorous, is central, but again, the self is not. The structure is often picaresque — meaning there is no continuous narrative but a series of events connected by the narrator. The personalities and stories of the people — or other creatures — the narrator meets form the heart of this kind of travel writing. An interesting cast of characters, well observed and enriched by interview and research, is the key element.

- *Personal journey writing*: chronicling self-discovery as much as discovery of another culture or place, for example, Robyn Davidson's *Desert Places*. There is a personal voice and perspective with the self at the centre of the narrative. It does not mean the writer is always looking inward or always writing about herself — that would almost certainly not be engaging — but it does mean the journey is given purpose by the desire for self-knowledge. There can be exploration of ideas — particularly spiritual ideas, cultures, individuals, geographical and historical place — but the central theme is the inner quest.

- *Sojourn writing*: traversing a period of time spent in one, often exotic, location, such as *Out of Africa* by Karen Blixen. Again, there is mostly a personal voice, but the self can either be the centre of the narrative or simply the observer. It is similar to the 'character' memoir in that individuals can be important, but often a process, such as restoring a farmhouse or setting up a café, provides a central narrative. An inner psychological or spiritual process can also provide the heart of the narrative. It is based on observation rather than research and is intensely subjective in its perspective.

- *Ideas writing*: exploring the history, culture, geography or politics of a foreign country, as William Dalrymple does in *The White Mughals*. Although there can be a personal voice, the self stands to one side. This type of travel memoir focuses on offering and exploring information. It demands a great deal of research as well as acute personal observation. You can focus on any area that interests you — anything from gypsy culture in Europe to the history of Bolivia. If you already have a particular area of interest and knowledge then a journey can make an appealing vehicle for you to explore and convey your passion.

This is not to say that your travel memoir needs to fit neatly into one of the above categories. It could turn out to be a mix of all of the above. Sarah Turnbull's *Almost French* is an adventure memoir in that she follows a Frenchman, whom she has only met once, to Paris, and is an ideas memoir in that it explores French culture and includes research and interviews. At the same time it is a sojourn memoir in that it explores her daily life in Paris and her process of becoming (almost) French. This list of memoir areas is simply a way for you to start thinking about the travel memoir you want to write.

The suitcase

You need to think about the size and type of your 'suitcase' — that is, how long your tale should be, and how it can be structured. Is it a short travel memoir, suitable for a travel anthology, or is it book length? Do your three weeks in

Nigeria warrant a book? Be ruthless about your material —
it may work well at 5000 words but become very thin at
book length. To misquote American columnist Russell
Baker, in *Inventing the Truth*, the desire to record one's travels
is no free pass to the reader's attention.

The structure of a travel memoir is normally chronological, dictated by the journey unfolding in time. You can
use the format of a diary, journal or letters to keep an orderly
chronology, or you can use seasons, places or incidents as
your markers. Chronology is easy to use and is an effective
first step in managing your material, but you need to be wary
of repetition. Your readers do not need to know every time
you see a glorious view over the Alps, or every time you stop
at a curious wayside inn.

You can just as well write a travel memoir which is not
chronological but organised, for example, around ideas, such
as VS Naipaul's exploration of the Islamic diaspora, *Beyond
Belief*, or based structurally on personalities, such as Susan
Varga and Anne Coombs' *Broomtime*, an account of a sojourn
in a small isolated town in northern Australia. These kinds of
memoir are more a vehicle for exploring concerns which are
not necessarily to do with travel, or at least not to do with
the physical act of travel. They are vehicles for inner journeys
of ideas or emotions.

Poetic and metaphoric images can be used as a way of
structuring your travel writing. A wonderful documentary,
The Gleaners and I, by French filmmaker Agnes Varda, uses a
series of original images, including paintings of gleaners, to
structure her travels around France. Because these images re-
occur, they unify the documentary and the viewer is struck
with the feeling that what is found by accident is a gift from
the universe and is to be treasured. A repeated image can be a
powerful way to connect events and thus structure a travel

memoir. Look to poetry, film and painting to find ways of patterning that convey the essence of your experience.

Read other travel memoirs and note the way they are put together, how the reader is moved from one place to another. In travel writing, you can arrive at a place without having to have stepped on board a plane or boat or train — unless, that is, the story happened on the plane or boat or train. In other words, to create the structure be ruthless about your journey, tell us what we need to know rather than recording everything you did.

What to pack

When you set off to write a travel memoir, bring to it all the same awareness, clarity and economy that you would bring to any memoir. Leave woolly perceptions, overworn phrases and shapeless generalisations in the wardrobe. Here are a few hints for a well-packed travel-writing suitcase.

• *A sharp, perceptive eye for what is original, fresh, illuminating.* Don't repeat descriptions of well-known sights. In this age of the image, everyone has seen a representation of everything already. Baudrillard, a French philosopher, called it 'the precession of the simulacra', that is, we are familiar with the image of the Eiffel Tower long before we see the actual tower. There is therefore no point in saying it is remarkably tall and elegant — everyone knows that. With your sharp eyes wide open, see instead the elderly Italian woman in high heels tottering up the steel steps of the tower trying to keep up with her grandchildren.

• *A sharp, perceptive eye for what is ordinary amongst the extraordinary.* It is often people going about the ordinary business of life which sheds most light on an 'exotic' place. And remember that what is exotic for you is ordinary for the people who live there. Try and see the marvel — the lake temple in Bali, or Mt Rushmore — as part of your daily life, and it will lose it gloss of 'difference' and you will be able to properly see and evoke it. For example, I was overwhelmed by the beauty and difference of Bali and was only able to write about the experience after I saw an old man lighting oil lamps around the rice fields with bats swarming in the gathering dusk above him. I realised this was ordinary life for him, not exotic, and I was then able to calmly write down what I saw without gushing clichés.

- *A selective judgment about what you include.* Don't write about every place you stayed, every meal you ate, every sight you visited, every peasant you met at the local market. You are not making a record or even a history of a journey or a place, you are re-creating the experience — or better still, you are creating a new experience based on your travels. You are taking the reader on a journey, inviting them to stay with you on your sojourn, but more than that, you are exploring the territory that interests everyone: the relationship between a person and his or her world.

- *Your own unique perception of people, events, places.* It is easy to fall into commonplace generalisations about the ever-present history of Europe or the grandeur of the United States or the greenness of Ireland. You are a distinctive person with your own education and experience so look at the world through your own awareness and reveal something new about it. Paris may always be Paris, but if you have a literary knowledge you will see a different Paris to someone who has an architectural or political or culinary knowledge. Each city, each place, is made anew by the people who experience it. Bring your own interests and knowledge to your travel writing.

- *Your own unique voice.* The voice of the narrator is just as important in travel memoir as it is in any other memoir — perhaps even more so, because the reader is alone in a foreign place with only you for company. You, as narrator, are our travelling companion and guide and we, the readers, want you to entertain, instruct, illuminate and keep us safe. You can make us laugh or cry, or amaze, startle or horrify us, but don't whinge, accuse or be dull.

- *A feeling for the meaning of your travels and sojourns.* It doesn't mean you need to know this from the beginning — why head off on a possibly perilous journey if you already know the answers? — but by the time you have redrafted your manuscript, there needs to be some sense of either an unfolding narrative or underlying meanings emerging. There doesn't have to be a cataclysmic climax or world-shattering insights, but a sense that this is more than just a record of what you did one year. You have opened up new territory somewhere in yourself and your world, and so in your reader.

- *Knowledge of local history and culture.* This will prevent you from writing extraordinarily foolish things. George Sand is not a Frenchman but a Frenchwoman; the Greek colonels were not just army officers but a military regime, The Whitlams in Australia are a rock band as well as a former prime minister and his family. And apart from preventing faux pas, the more you know about a place, the richer your travel writing will be. Do your research.

- *Sensitivity to religious and cultural difference.* This is that offence can be minimised. It is not that you must agree that everything about the religion or culture is wonderful, but knowledge of why people carry out various practices and rituals can make your writing more interesting, less patronising and less judgmental.

- *An awareness of 'reverse racism'.* Everything about a people different from your own can become charming, friendly, sunny, innocent but racial clichés, however benign, are always patronising — perhaps all Fijians can sing, all Balinese can dance, but it is a cultural, rather than a racial characteristic. The same goes for generalised national characteristics — they are neither useful nor true. Not all Frenchwomen are chic, not all Americans are gregarious, not all English people are reserved and not all Italians are passionate.

- *A sensual awareness of place.* Notice new smells, sounds, textures and tastes as well as sights. A new place is a new experience for the senses as well as for the mind, and even when your writing is focused on cultural, historical or political concerns, it will be more powerful if the senses are also engaged. Ground your thoughts in the senses — in the smell of coriander cooking, the colour of emerald silk saris, the sight of cow dung on the heel of a businessman's shoe.

- *Original words and phrases.* These should know how to behave themselves, meaning they know how to sit quietly and do their work rather than shout noisily. They must be fresh, not tired, obvious and overused (no *gorgeous* Alpine sunsets) and not excessively elaborate (no *roseate blush on ebony skins of Mali maidens*) — unless you are being satiric of hyperbolic style, that is. Take every type of cliché out of the suitcase and put it back in the wardrobe. You will not need *beckoned at every turn,* or *tropical paradise* or *fabled ruined city.* Better still, take the clichés out and put them in the bin — you have never needed them and will not ever need them.

- *Take out long static descriptions of places or people.* That is, get rid of descriptions in which nothing happens. Even if you are simply writing about a still pond, observe the dancing movement of dragonflies, the croaking of frogs, the shivering of a morning wind on the surface of the water. Be wary of overlong, overindulgent descriptions of anything.

- *In a side 'suitcase' include journals, notes, letters, postcards, emails you kept at the time.* Read them with critical eyes — they were probably most often written to reassure family and friends, and yourself, that you were indeed having a good time, and so are probably full of generalisations and hyperbole. They can, however, serve to locate times and places that might have blurred in your memory. Journals can also be useful for bringing back people and scenes which were important at the time but which memory has filtered out. Generally it is not a good idea to quote directly from these sources because even if the writing is precise and evocative, the narrating voice is probably very different from your voice now. Use the material, but rewrite it.

- *Pack novels and memoirs by other good writers on the same topics.* The point of this is not to make you feel it has all been done already and that you ought to give up, but so that you can be inspired to go further. We all, at times, require a draught of some consciousness — expanding words from a truly inspiring writer to help us take that extra step off the ground and into flight.

The travel or sojourn memoir is often thought of as more glamorous than everyday memoir. It includes exotic locations and all the natural attractions of life outside the ordinary: the kinds of places and experiences people dream about at their desks or kitchen sinks. But it still requires discipline, clarity and attention to detail. Essentially, what is interesting is your perception of, and relation to, the environment. Alain de Botton said in *The Art of Travel*, 'I had inadvertently brought myself with me to the island.' We all do that — and that is what makes travel memoir interesting. The island remains more or less the same; each perception of it is different.

READING

True Pleasures: A Memoir of Women in Paris

by Lucinda Holdforth

I thread my way across to a corner café, Ma Bourgogne, where I order a glass of soft red wine, and settle down to watch and to daydream. I am gazing at the present, but I am thinking about the past. Here, I think, *here*, is where it all began.

When foreigners want to understand the French, they generally head to Versailles. That's because at Versailles, it is said, Louis XIV, the Sun King himself, invented French culture. He commenced renovations on a family hunting lodge in 1661, and he progressively moved the court there from Paris from about 1674. Louis XIV made Versailles a gilded cage for his captive aristocrats. He kept the ruling class entirely occupied with pleasure and ceremony: he made his courtiers so busy they had neither time nor inclination to plot against him. The Sun King established an elaborate social code, which, through war and conquest, he exported to the rest of Europe. But Louis XIV didn't invent French culture; he just borrowed it.

Over here on my left is number 20 Place des Vosges. This is where a bride arrived from Italy to stay in the house of her father-in-law, sometime around 1590. Her name was Catherine de Vivonne, the new Marquise de Rambouillet. From courtly Italy with its chivalrous traditions she had landed in rough-hewn France. Place des Vosges, then known as Place Royale, was still under construction. Its primary use was as a rowdy military parade ground. Residents woke at dawn to the metal clashes of duellists fighting for sport or honour. Life in Paris was altogether medieval and martial. *Worst of all,* thought the young bride, *the houses*! Grand homes were designed like feudal hunting lodges, with draughty baronial spaces and blood red walls.

So la Marquise commissioned a house, a perfect house. Her blue, white and gold reception room was intimate, scaled down, with little alcoves to encourage private exchanges. La Marquise, in her lilting Italian accent, called the reception space her *salone*, and it became, of course, the first salon. The guest list was pruned to privilege talent, beauty, honour and wit: only the greatest artists and writers were invited; the bravest soldiers; the most beautiful pious women. Wives and husbands were not automatically included — no free riders, thanks — and this no doubt contributed a flirtatious element to the conversation. For the first time, women became socially central. Their role was to guide, to instruct, to inspire, to elevate — the most refined were known as *les précieuses*. Men aspired to become *honnêtes hommes* — honourable, cultivated, natural and, most important of all, socially graceful. At the core of this little society was a new idea — the art of living itself, *savoir vivre*.

Under one roof, la Marquise de Rambouillet brought together all the elements we associate with Paris today: the elevation to art of food, conversation, clothes and love. The historian Vincent Cronin said of Place Royale: *This square can be said to mark the change from the rough masculine society of Henry IV to the witty society revolving around certain gifted or beautiful women which still prevails today.*

Just over on the other side of the square at number 1 is the birthplace of la Marquise de Rambouillet's most famous guest, Madame de Sévigné. Madame de Sévigné sparkled. She was funny, spirited and worldly. Later she lived around the corner in what is now Musée Carnavalet, appropriately the museum of Paris history. Her letters embody the French idea of *esprit* — wit, intellect and spirit combined.

Time for another wine, and now I look directly across the square to where it exits to rue du Pas de la Mule. Just around the corner lived the most influential courtesan of the seventeenth century. She used to ride into this square on a little sedan-chair carried by her menservants. Her name was Ninon de Lanclos.

Ninon de Lanclos wasn't like the *précieuses*: she wasn't elevated or precious. She was an epicurean — a philosopher of judicious pleasure. *All good sense should lead in the direction of happiness*, she believed. Unlike the pious women of la Marquise de Rambouillet's salon, Ninon demanded all the liberties and responsibilities available to men. Her motto was: *Make me a gentle man* (honnête homme), *but never a chaste woman* ...

One of Ninon's early admirers was Cardinal Richelieu. He lived here in Place Royale too, at number 21 — just behind me in fact, and, see, there's a plaque on the shopfront. He offered Ninon a fortune to become his mistress. She declined: the outrageous sum of money was too much from a lover but not enough from a man she didn't love.

As she matured, Ninon became so respectable
that society ladies would send their sons to study at her
school of gallantry. We can thank Ninon for the
Frenchman's romantic reputation: she turned gauche
young men into ardent and skilful lovers. *It takes a hundred
times more skill to make love than to command an army,* she
used to say.

True Pleasures is a travel memoir of ideas, shaped around an
exploration of Paris as a city formed by women. Holdforth
sets out on a personal journey through the lives, loves and
attitudes of celebrated Parisienne women, aligning their lives
with her own. Read this literary travel memoir to see how
Holdforth has blended her personal journey with a well-
researched and engaging view of a much-inscribed city.

WRITING EXERCISES

1. Memento

Take a memento from a particular journey — a postcard or
souvenir — and use it as a springboard to start writing. This
is not an exercise in description — simply use the memento
as a concrete way to focus your mind. Do not plan what you
are going to write about, simply look at the memento for a
couple of minutes, then begin. *(15 minutes)*

2. Backgrounds

Take a photograph from a particular place and look at something in the image other than the main subject. See what
else is in the photo — the young mother on rollerskates in
the corner of your picture of the Seine, for example. Use the

'background' detail as a way in to writing about that day or that place. *(20 minutes)*

3. Research

Go on the Internet or visit a library and do some research on the countries or cities you want to write about. The research can be historical, political, cultural — or in any other arca that interests you. Try weaving the research into the story of your travels there, rewriting the information in your own words.

4. Senses

Write, in note form, five different sensory impressions of a place you have been to, one impression for each sense — sight, sound, taste, smell and touch. Beginning with one of the senses, evoke the place using all the senses. Remember that static writing is generally less interesting than writing in which something happens. *(5 minutes for each sense)*

5. Playing with structure

Write five distinct short pieces, half a page each, about a journey you have taken or a place you have stayed, each piece about a different aspect of the same journey or sojourn. Each one must show in detail an event or place or person, and self-contained, not consciously linked to or referring to the other pieces. Think of this exercise as a series of 'close-ups' where one can see the beard on the oyster in the café in Le Conquet. When you have finished, read through them and play with arranging them in relation to each other. See which order best re-creates your experience. Do you need to write more pieces? See whether you can build up a longer piece — say 5000 words — using this method. *(15 minutes for each piece)*

6. Truthful postcards

Next time you are away from home, try writing a completely truthful postcard. (You don't have to post it.)

11.
RANDOM
PROVOCATIONS —
THE PERSONAL ESSAY

AT UNIVERSITY I was one of those odd students who actually liked writing essays. It's shameful, I know — such a solitary indulgence should not have been given in to — but now that I spend much of my life in this activity, I may as well admit that I enjoyed the teasing out of an idea, the propounding of a theory, the pulling together of various threads, the searching for words to say it all.

You will notice, however, that I have left out 'research'. I did not enjoy research. The relevant textbooks had always been borrowed from the library already by far more organised and diligent students than I, it took ages to find anything useful in the odd, out-of-date texts left on the shelves, and when I did find something, I invariably failed to record the publication details for the footnotes and had to spend hours re-finding the scraps of information before the essay could be handed in. Even now, when there is endless availability of research sources on the Internet, part of me still resists the plunge into the sea of information and facts.

Ay, there's the rub. The truth of the matter is that I do not have a passionate interest in, nor respect for, the facts. Fortunately for all concerned, I recognised this flaw in my character early on — indeed, before leaving high school. Although I achieved decent marks in the sciences, it was clear that I did not have sufficient respect for the facts to make a good scientist. Indeed, I would have been one of those reprehensible scientists who invent data to support the wonderful theory they have concocted.

It's not that I don't like facts per se. A few fascinating facts are necessary, even pleasurable, but my overruling passion is the mad leap from the fact into the 'grand idea'. (Mine are not so very grand, more small meditations on odd fragments of middling ideas, but you know what I mean.) I like to circle around the idea, stretch it out, wriggle it about, snap it back, tease it out again and give it a good shake. That is why the endlessly elastic form of the personal essay is perfect — with only a fact or two in my possession, I can stretch and wriggle and tease to my heart's content.

The personal essay is related to the academic or formal essay in that both explore ideas, but an academic essay requires that you have information and research and facts at your command. A personal essayist does not command anything; he wanders with great attention across the topic, regarding everything with wonder. A formal academic essay also demands objectivity — you are required to leave yourself out of the situation. A personal essayist is the opposite: she looks at everything from her own subjective point of view, and will often even tell stories about herself.

The personal essayist has something to say but is not quite sure what. She is like a Messenger who doesn't know what the message is, who it is from, or where it is going. But she feels if she wanders around with it long enough, stares at it often enough, she will decipher what it is saying and where it needs to be delivered.

You may say that the personal essay is an excuse for every kind of intellectual laziness and self-indulgence, and maybe it is, but it is very charming at the same time. And it has the added advantage, in my eyes, of being closely related to memoir. If it is the academic essay's disreputable, eccentric cousin, then it is also the memoir's intellectually playful sibling and the child of confession — an expression of the urge to note as truthfully as possible the gap between the dream we have of ourselves, and what we actually are.

Genealogy

It sounds oxymoronic to say so, but it is often dull and dangerous to name 'important people' in any field. Dull because a list of names — without room for explanation or narrative — is unexciting, and dangerous because of the ire of those who know how many names have been left off the list. Still, a list also provides somewhere to start for the would-be essayist, an introduction to the complex extended family of the personal essay.

Where did the essay come from? *Essai* was the name given by the sixteenth century French writer Michel de Montaigne to his own style of writing — short explorations of himself in relation to his world. He took the word from the French *essayer*, meaning 'to try' or 'to attempt'. He was attempting to know himself and thereby know humankind, believing that 'Every man has within himself the entire human condition'.

Although he was the first writer to devote himself to it in post-Renaissance Europe, Montaigne did not invent the personal essay. At the beginning of the first millennium, the early Romans Seneca and Plutarch were writing essays; and in the tenth century in Japan, Sei Shonagon wrote her famous *Pillow Book*. Around the same time in China, Ou-yang Hsiu let his 'brush write what it would'. In the early fourteenth century, Kenko, also Japanese, wrote *The Tseurezuregusa*, the original title of which comes from the expression 'with nothing better to do'.

The English personal essay had a famous flowering in the eighteenth and nineteenth centuries with such names as Addison, Steele, Johnson, Lamb, Hazlitt and Robert Louis Stevenson. The tradition was kept up in the early twentieth century by English and American writers: GK Chesterton, Max Beerbohm, Virginia Woolf, George Orwell, Walter Benjamin, Henry Thoreau, EB White and James Thurber. Later in the century and into the twenty-first century, the form has been kept alive by, amongst others, Joan Didion, Annie Dillard, Jorge Luis Borges, Roland Barthes and Robert Dessaix. To read extracts from any or all of these writers' works, look in Phillip Lopate's wonderful — in fact indispensable — collection, *The Art of the Personal Essay*.

Substance

As Ou-yang Hsiu said, a personal essayist lets his brush write what it will. It is the literary form for the writer with an attic mind — everything is stored there, trash and treasure, and in no particular order. Your topic can be anything you find in that attic, often the smaller and less regarded, the better. Walter

Benjamin wrote about the different ways one acquires books, a delight to anyone who is a compulsive acquirer of books, but not of world-shaking importance. I once wrote an essay on how to select a book-companion when travelling in foreign lands, again a topic of no great import. But in writing about the small, the daily, the ignored, the essayist is making a democratic claim for the wonder and complexity of all of life.

Wander into the attic or labyrinth of your mind and notice what is there. Not your large concerns about violence and peace, poverty and injustice, but the smaller, daily observations: the eternal battle between the tidy and the messy; the embarrassment people feel when they trip in public; the pleasures of obscure knowledge; the irritation of eternal cheeriness; the way people purse their mouths when they look in mirrors. In the hands of a personal essayist, these humble topics become an exploration of aspects of the human condition. GK Chesterton wrote about the foolishness a man feels when he is chasing his hat and it becomes a light but sharp meditation on the general absurdity of much of life.

However light the topic appears, there is always the struggle for truthfulness. Personal essayists oppose falseness, flattery, prudery, priggishness — any kind of dishonesty about the self. The American essayist EB White, quoted in *The Art of the Personal Essay*, wrote, 'There is one thing the essayist cannot do — he cannot indulge himself in deceit or in concealment, for he will be found out in no time.' The essayist makes himself vulnerable and his best protection is truthfulness.

The personal essay is very ecologically sound because it is a way of using everything you know, of recycling every little scrap, not letting anything go to waste. That difficult book by a French writer you once read, that item you noted in the newspaper, your knowledge of odd historical facts, that childhood memory, the remark your son once made — they all connect to your subject. Thus, in finding a topic, what matters is that it has lain in the attic for a while. It must have gathered to itself various connections and associations. Perhaps it seems like a new thought — you have suddenly noticed the etiquette of pointing out scraps of food on someone's face when out at restaurants, for example — but once you notice the new thought, you become aware that it has numerous associations. This, for me, is the test of a good topic — if, once you start tugging on it, a whole jumble of things comes falling out, landing on your head and clattering to the floor, then it is a good topic.

Voice

Now that you are standing there stunned, or perhaps knocked down into a foolish position by the assortment of material you have uncovered, you can hardly look or sound earnest and dignified about the matter. Carrying off this situation requires attitude. The personal essay is all about attitude — expressed as *voice*.

The voice of the personal essayist is often conversational, playful, confiding, amused. It can be serious but not plodding, nor complacent. If you are, by nature, self-satisfied and very sure about everything, then you possibly will not be a good essayist. As Montaigne suggested, an essayist is trying something, he is not sure. You can reveal your ignorance, your folly, your faults, not with a self-pitying desire for forgiveness, but with a humorous shrug — this is the way we all are. This questioning, intimate voice can be gently humorous, acerbic, world-weary, mock-bossy or as tender as Virginia Woolf writing about a moth fluttering to death against a window, but not earnest or pontificating. Nor is self-righteousness permitted, except to the ironic essayist who can do whatever he chooses.

The personal essayist can be as intimate and as subjective as she likes. An open frankness about topics not permitted in general conversation — anything from bodily functions to schadenfreude — can be very winning, allowing the reader to recognise her own thoughts and giving the curious pleasure of stripping away illusion, of seeing oneself in someone else's mirror. You can even be frank to the point of shock — so long as it doesn't destroy the reader's trust in you. Be as cheeky, humorous, ironic as you like. You can also be as contrary as you like — a personal essayist thrives on contrariness. Phillip Lopate wrote a piece called 'Against Joie de Vivre', and manages to convincingly win the reader over to what looks at first like a curmudgeonly world view.

The essay is held together by the charm of the narrator, the 'I'. Conversational language is part of the charm. The essayists will say things like 'You might object' and 'Of course, you know' — and the reader feels included in the conversation because she is being addressed. This is the pleasure and the danger of the essay. It is pleasant for the reader to feel confided in, often flattering to feel herself the recipient of considered thoughts, but there is the danger of the egotistical 'I' — crowding the reader.

The secret is to realise, in whatever you say as an essayist, that you are speaking not just for yourself. An essayist uses 'I' but, in a sense, she is really saying 'we'. In fact, the 'I' is also sometimes modulated to 'we' or 'you', or for the more polite and correct essayists, 'one'. This is a way of including the reader more closely, of acknowledging the reader as part of the conversation. A mixture of pronouns can work, but be careful not to be too random about who is speaking and who is listening.

At the same time, you have the chance to hold the floor, to be as witty and quick as you like with no one to interrupt you. It's not a matter of 'trying hard' to be clever — it's all about sitting back in the armchair or on the canvas chair on the balcony and relaxing with your idea.

The personal essayist is the perfect host, letting everything happen without seeming to do anything. He appears to be an idler, a wanderer, an onlooker; no one realises he has instigated the whole affair. He doesn't rush about rearranging the furniture or organising anybody or making big speeches. He wanders quietly looking at things in the living room or out in the street or office or forest, and then idly begins to turn these things over in his mind.

The essayist agrees with RL Stevenson, who said, 'Extreme busyness ... is a symptom of deficient vitality ... They (who cannot be idle) have no curiosity; they cannot give themselves to random provocations.'

Holding it together

If the voice of the idler — sorry, essayist — is that of an intriguing, challenging, amusing onlooker, it also provides the thread which holds the whole essay together. The voice of the 'I' and its characteristic attitudes and expressions creates the essayist's 'persona', the strongest single element of an essay's structure. The essayist cultivates aspects of himself — often a flaw such as a waywardness or clumsiness — and makes it an identifying part of his writing persona. The American essayist James Thurber, for example, cultivated the persona of someone with a very short attention span, afflicted with 'the permanent jumps' as his great aunt used to say.

Throughout the various 'random provocations', the strong persona holds the reader's attention, maintains a consistent perspective, wins the reader back if the challenges have been a little difficult. The persona needs to be flexible enough to move from gossip to wisdom and back again without jarring. The persona can address the reader, ask questions, challenge — in fact, be an engaging and interesting friend.

While an engaging persona is a necessity, it is not necessarily all. It is not a guarantee that you won't end up with a ramble only marginally more interesting than Uncle Stan's mishmash of tales that lasted all afternoon at a family get-together last weekend. An essayist may use the same techniques as Uncle Stan — circling, digressing, meandering — but uses them consciously, always reaching towards some overall purpose. While an essayist might seem at times to be wandering off the point, he is actually elaborating, refining, teasing out.

The art of elaboration is a delicate one. It is not to be mistaken for mere embroidery, although I must say I have nothing against a little well-done embroidery — it can be very pretty. Elaboration, on the other hand, does not add pretty details, but unfolds, untangles, dismantles, what is already there. The personal essayist likes to pull out the tangle bit by bit, following various threads, finding origins and possible implications. This can involve examples, lists, quotes, historical references, anecdotes, personal history. It can be done step-by-step, but the essayist generally digresses and circles, moving from a childhood memory to yesterday's item in the newspaper to a quote from Freud — bit by bit unfolding the whole curious piece of cloth.

While I am being metaphorical, it might also help to think of the structuring of an essay as a kaleidoscope. A kaleidoscope breaks up the usual scene into many tiny pieces, but because of its inner geometry, puts the bits together in a new and rhythmic way. The essayist puts the bits of her world together in a new way so that the familiar is refreshed.

Or again, think of the essay as a 'walkabout', the Australian Aboriginal practice of breaking away from the restrictions of daily life and heading off into the wilderness for a period of renewal. Collect what you see as you go and hold it together with the shape and idea of the journey itself.

The essayist also tells tales. And I mean *tells*. Here is where you can ignore EM Forster's maxim, 'Show, don't tell', for the essayist tells everything they know, have seen, have heard other people say. As an essayist, you are a scavenger of anecdote, family tales, memories, all told in your own way to serve the purposes of your essay.

You can use knowledge gleaned from formal education as well. If you know about the making of copper, or the theories of Jung, or the history of European painting, or quotes from Wittgenstein, then let them find their place in your structure. This is not to show how erudite you are, but odd knowledge is part of the eclectic nature of the essay. The essayist is never too proud to think that other people have not said it better than he can. Even our hero, Montaigne, wrote, 'For I make others say what I cannot say so well, now through the weakness of my language, now through the weakness of my understanding.' The trick is in creating an atmosphere of easy access to learning through the conversational voice, which will allow you to use such quotes or extracts without appearing pretentious.

Play, free-associate — these are your formal practices when you write a personal essay. I nearly said 'sit down to write', but I invariably find that I begin personal essays when I am out strolling. There is something about the easy movement of walking and the changing scenery that creates a model of the personal essay. It is not a static form, nor even a pre-existing form; it is found in movement, in play. Start writing because an idea or observation interests you, then follow any connections or associations as they arise.

The essayist needs to be a trusting creature, both in terms of pursuing ideas and finding structure. The essay is not a definite form, like a sonnet, nor is it even as recognisable as a short story, so you need to believe that you can head off into uncharted territory with no precise destination — and still get there. I usually start by jotting down some of the main landmarks, with no real idea of where I will end up, but somehow I always do know when I've got to wherever it was I was going. There is always an 'epiphany' as James Joyce called it, the *aha* moment — aha, this is where I meant to get to all the time.

How long one can permit oneself to wander is a question that needs to be faced. Personally, I find it fairly easy to decide — I stop when I am done, when I have got to my destination. It is much easier than deciding when a short story or a memoir or novel is done. There is an inevitability about the end of an essay which is easy to recognise. In some sense, I have an idea before I start that this will be a short wander, perhaps 1000 to 1500 words, or a long wander, 3000 to 5000 words. Of course, there are book length wanders as well, but these are generally made up of a number of shorter journeys.

While there may be a series of small revelations throughout the essay, its full meaning is not usually revealed until the conclusion — probably because the essayist herself did not know the answer until she got there. This is the delight of the essay; you really are trying something out, you do not know where you are going to get to. If you already know, there is nothing to try, no *essai*. You are working not with a pre-existing shape, not with a whole monolithic form, but

a form which can endlessly break into smaller pieces and re-
form, like pieces of mercury fallen on a table. And Mercury,
after all, was the messenger of the gods.

READING

Get the drift

by Patti Miller

Choosing the right book to take with you on your travels
in another country is a delicate matter — it being a given
that you want to take a book to read, not just a travel
guide. It's a bit like choosing the right travelling companion;
you don't want to arrive and then find your book likes to
party every night while you want to gaze meditatively at
temples in the moonlight, or conversely, your book wants
to think deeply about the meaning of the Tao, and you
plan to loll sensuously under the coconut palms.

Clearly, the right travelling companion book will be in
tune with your experience and will heighten and interact
with it. It will also have the capacity to refresh when you
have become weary, give strength when you're coming
undone, and hopefully, give you perspective when you're
feeling ill-tempered with the difficulty of everybloody-
thing in this damn country.

The logical method for selection is to find a book
which relates to your destination: if you are travelling in
Canada, then Margaret Atwood or Alice Munro; if South
America, then Isabel Allende, Gabriel Garcia Marquez,
Jorge Luis Borges; if San Francisco, then Armistead
Maupin, or if Dublin, then James Joyce. But there is a
chemistry between person and place and book which can
be unpredictable. You don't really know how you will react

in a certain place, nor how you will react to your book-companion in such a place.

That's why I suggest the Slow Drift Method of Book Selection, which I came upon after a few false, and faulty, choices. The Slow Drift is a traditional time-honoured method, its origins lost in the dust of libraries past (I make no claims to having invented it), which, with a little practice, can be used by anyone. It requires the application of a slow, deep, almost non-attention — the Drift. Then, and only then, will you be able to discern the unspoken intuitive level of connection you need with a true companion.

The way to apply the Slow Drift is to stand in front of your own bookcase or in a library or bookshop and slowly walk up and down, looking at the covers of the books but not thinking about anything. When you sense any stirring in the region of your solar plexus (the area under your ribs), take the book in front of you down, open it and read a sentence or two. If the words correspond with the sensation in your solar plexus, then this is the right book. If not, then return to the Slow Drift. It is very simple.

Using this method you can still end up with the same book as the logical method. For instance, for my first trip to Paris, it didn't take much Drifting at all to choose Colette's *Rainy Moon*. Although, when you think about it, why was Colette any more logical a companion than dozens of others? What about Balzac for some historical realism, or Barthes for a dose of semiotics, or Anaïs Nin for the claustrophobic narcissism of the Artist? Or the Paris-Americans — Edith Wharton, Henry James, Henry Miller, Gertrude Stein …

But, the Slow Drift had resulted in Colette, so I put *Rainy Moon* in my bag. The choice was rewarded even as

I flew over the Timor Sea. When I came to the line 'I found myself possessed of a more provident attitude for dealing with improvidence', I laughed out loud and knew that Colette and I would have a superb time in Paris.

Sometimes the Drift results in a choice which seems illogical altogether. A few years ago I was making a sentimental journey back to New Zealand — as a young woman setting out to see the world more than a few years ago, I had hopped across the Tasman Sea, lived in a commune on the Coromandel Peninsula for several months, had a child, and not seen much of the rest of the world for too many years. I'd not wanted to return, fearing I would be caught again in New Zealand's damp green embrace, but now I was old enough, nostalgic enough, to want to visit my lost youth.

I was also in the middle of writing a novel and needed some distance from it, a forced separation. I was feeling my way in the dark with it, not knowing where or how the story would finish but trying to trust that it was going somewhere. When the Slow Drift method resulted in *Leaning Towards Infinity,* Sue Woolfe's novel of 'mathematics and motherhood', I couldn't see how it connected to either my communal past or my present need. And Woolfe had given me the book to read in manuscript form. How could I treat it as a companion when I had seen it partially formed, undressed, made intimate comments about it to its creator? I thought the Drift must be wrong. I moved along to New Zealand writers, to my old love, Katherine Mansfield. But there was no silent response under my demanding gaze. It was no use; *Infinity* it was.

It flew to Christchurch with me, accompanied me through the wild autumn mountains around Queenstown, traversed the deep mysteries of the fiords, wandered along the edges of milky jade lakes and was an agreeable companion, but not an intimate one. Then one night we stayed at Mount Aoarangi, the Cloud Piercer, and a snowstorm blew in as we lay snug in bed. I went to sleep with the snow and wind swirling past the window.

In the middle of that dark night, a line from *Infinity* suddenly woke me. *It seems, she'd say, as if humans have been prepared for something other than survival.* I lay awake with the sentence, the wind howling, the snow gusting, seeing my own youth here, and the half-finished novel at home, small streams in the ancient flood of yearning for 'something other than survival' which has so distressed us all. I felt pierced, as if by a kind of avenging angel's sword, woken up to the mystery of existence. There is no better service a book-companion can give.

The Drift method of selection is a very subtle thing, however. The ego is always trying to take charge and can even imitate the Drift. It happened last year when I found myself organising to go to Bali. I didn't really know why I was going — I did need a break but I knew it was western indulgence to go so far just to relax. And I felt snobbishly embarrassed at going to a tourist trap with so many fellow Australians.

In this frame of mind, I chose *The God of Small Things*. I had already started reading it and knew that for my taste Arundhati Roy's writing was over-lush, probably overwrought, but thought that this would be in tune with a Hindu tropical island. It was also a beautiful-looking book with an intriguing title, so it would signal that I wasn't a typical Oz yob lying around the resort pool. It's exactly this kind of snobbery and pretension which pollutes the Drift, and even as it was packed, I had a sense that this was not going to be my true companion.

At the airport bookshop I used the Slow Drift again
and found myself holding Robert Dessaix's *Night Letters*.
Rationally, it didn't seem the right book at all — it was set
in northern Italy — but instantly I knew that this was my
true book-companion. I started reading as we flew and
was excited and calmed (both at once is possible — all
good literature does it) by his eye on the world. I read
of his meeting with a well-dressed middle-aged woman
on a train as he headed into northern Italy, and was
reminded of two well-dressed middle-aged women
I had watched folding tea-towels into bon-bon and
flower shapes on a train from Venice years ago. As
these elegant women created tea-towel kitsch on the
train, I had experienced an overwhelmingly delicious
shivery sensation down my spine, a more intense
experience than any of the marvels I'd seen in Venice
had induced. It was the electricity of really noticing
the every-day.

The 'woman on the train' image jolted me into
wakefulness, but all during the days and nights in Bali, as
sacred and sensuous as one could desire, even with the
noise, traffic and hawkers breeding on us pale tourists,
Night Letters continued to be the perfect companion. Each
evening I watched a Balinese man light oil lamps on stakes
around the rice paddies to keep the mosquitoes away; in
the dim light, bats swooped over the rice, darting with
more jagged movements than birds. These were the
ordinary things of daily life on Bali. When you are
travelling it's easy to become jaded with the accumulation
of marvels you are witnessing, to forget that you are seeing
the ordinary things of other people's daily lives.

Like all good companions, *Night Letters* reminded me of
the exultation of truly 'bearing witness', observing and

considering each moment; the moment when the masseuse plucked a stray marigold petal from my oiled body; when the backs of the *kecak* dancers gleamed in the moonlight; when the spicy meal I had at lunch time came up in a brilliant orange curve as I trod water on a coral reef. Of course, this last is stretching the demands you can make on a companion, but even so, a kind companion will tolerate the mess and even confess their own moments of disorder.

Disorder and alienation and losing direction are part of travel, along with joy and revelation. I am at a point in my life where I have no particular journeys planned, or rather, don't have any clear idea of what direction to take next. A number of times in his travels across Italy, Dessaix offers the idea of following at random an unknown person so that conscious choice and decision are subverted, a kind of giving way to the forces of the universe. This is what I mean by the Drift as a method of choosing — a submission, at least for a moment, to what the world has to offer you. It really is the best way to select a travel book.

In this newspaper essay, advice on how to select a travel book becomes a metaphor for the philosphical notion of living in the moment. It maintains a light conversational tone — *I had hopped across the Tasman* — but manages at the same time to explore existential themes — *woken up to the mystery of existence*. The idea of the 'book-companion' holds the essay together.

WRITING EXERCISES

1. A week's worth of thoughts

Write a list of the things you would think about in a week. Your list needs to be democratic and non-judgmental — that is, include things you may consider shallow as well as your intellectual or aesthetic thoughts. Include anything from choosing which shoes to wear, to the passage you read in Proust. Select one from the list and see if it starts pulling other associations out with it. Jot down whatever you think of in relation to it. Write a paragraph for each association. *(30 minutes)*

2. Another week's worth

Write a list of the things you might think about in a week. As above, your list needs to include anything and everything — do not screen for suitability. This time, write about as many of the topics as you can, using as your central idea 'the things I think about in a week'. Imagine it as a journey through your mind over a week— try it out. See where it goes — perhaps it will yield a new insight into life. Perhaps not. *(1 hour)*

3. Hateful things

Write a list of 'hateful things' — things that annoy or irritate you generally or in any particular situation. It could be a list of things that irritate you at parties, or in lifts, or at the hairdresser's. Write a paragraph on each and see if they join up to become an essay on the minor difficulties of being human. *(30 minutes)*

4. Mirror

Look at yourself in a metaphorical mirror. Notice something characteristic in the way that you think or go about things. It could be anything from the way you love idiosyncratic or useless information to the way you always tidy the apartment when your mother is coming to visit although you are a grown woman yourself. See if you can use this observation as a way of exploring an aspect of yourself and others. Jot down associations such as other people you have observed with this same trait, scientific research on the trait, literary connections, news items — anything in the attic of your mind. Try out the various associations and see where it leads you. *(30 minutes)*

12.

BORDERLANDS —
MEMOIR AND
FICTION

AT A WRITERS' festival in Australia a few years ago, I was on a discussion panel titled 'The Memoir Writer's Responsibility to the Truth' alongside a woman who had written about the 'honour killing' of her friend. According to her memoir, they had grown up together in Jordan and had opened a hairdressing salon as young women. Her friend was lively, warm, and had fallen in love with a boy her parents would not have approved of. Of course, they were found out, and even though their love had only been expressed in hand-holding and one or two brief kisses, she was 'honour killed' by her father and brothers. As I read the memoir, I felt anger at the distortion of the concept of honour, incomprehension at such familial violence for an idea, grief at the loss of a young life, admiration for the woman who had so courageously set down the story of herself and her friend. The memoir was not particularly well written, but it seemed churlish and nit-picking in the extreme to think of such literary considerations in the face of the horror she had experienced.

The problem was, a few weeks after the festival it was discovered that none of the key elements of her story were true. The author had, in fact, grown up not in Jordan, but in Chicago, and none of her friends had been 'honour-killed'. It did seem to be true that she was a hairdresser ...

More recently, there have been other memoirists who have written about lives of terrible tragedy, abuse, addiction, only for it to be discovered — after the 'memoirs' had sold extremely well — that most of the experiences were invented.

There was, of course, outrage at the deception each time, followed by debate about the differences between memoir and fiction. These cases highlighted the reality that, despite post-modernist realisations of truth as a construction, there is an accepted relationship of trust between a memoirist and a reader, mirroring the trust between friends. We are, as a rule, not post-modernist in our interpretation of our personal conversations. If a friend tells us they were hit by their father as a child, we accept that is what happened. We may question the friend's interpretation of the event, but we do not question that it truly happened.

In the same way, the memoirist affirms, I am telling you something important about myself, which you can believe actually occurred. This assumption of truth is as fundamental to memoir as it is to friendship, but even so, there are many areas in which even the most factual of memoirists might need to use the techniques of fiction. It is worth exploring the borderlands between the two and finding out what parts of the territory you feel able to inhabit. How far can you go in memoir, and still feel you are telling the truth of your experience?

Fiction in memoir

Many successful memoirs have used what might be fairly judged as fictional techniques:

- *Invented dialogue*. If someone makes a remark which is particularly tender and loving — or particularly cutting for that matter — you will probably remember the exact wording but, generally, most of us cannot remember exactly what we ourselves said yesterday, let alone what other people said many years ago. Yet you do want to create the lived texture of life on the page and you cannot do that without some use of dialogue. You will need to 'make up' what was said. Most people accept that the memoirist has remembered only the gist and is making up the actual dialogue, keeping in mind the characteristic way in which a person spoke. In a sense, you are using invention, but it is grounded in your memory.

  Then there are conversations at which you were not present, but which you know took place. In *Angela's Ashes*, Frank McCourt details a conversation between his father and his aunts that happened before he was born! Does the reader feel deceived? It seems to me that most readers in this situation accept the fact that they are being told a good story; they know, too, that he could not have heard the conversation, so they accept a little artistic licence. The intent is not to deceive, but to illuminate.

- *Imagining lives from a few facts*. It has become increasingly popular in family memoirs to imagine the lives of long gone or absent family members. Strictly speaking, this is not memoir at all — memoir is remembered, not imagined — but such imagining has become part of memoir in practice. In Gaby Naher's *The Truth About My*

Fathers, she imagines the lives of grandparents from a few spare facts; this is the realm of fiction, but the book is subtitled a memoir. It is a legitimate literary device — it can give an emotional richness and a lived texture to otherwise bare and dusty family history, and it seems to me that the trust with the reader is not broken because it is clear that the writer has again used artistic licence.

- *Imagined inner lives*. Clearly, the memoirist has no special access to the inner lives of family members and friends. She can deduce feelings and perceptions from what is said and done, but cannot with certainty know the mental and emotional life which produced them. Yet some memoirists create the inner reality of other people in their lives, either by describing or evoking them or by some device such as an invented diary. In *Poppy*, Drusilla Modjeska invents the diaries of her mother to give the reader access to her mother's inner life. The reader may not be aware at first that the diaries are imagined, but Modjeska states in the dedication at the front of the book, 'To my mother, who never kept a diary'. This memoir then is partly fiction. It is a slightly different genre — read as memoir/biography, that is, with the belief that it is true, but with awareness that some of it, based on the outward facts, is imagined. Whether you want to try such techniques is up to you, but it's important to remember not to break the trust the reader has in your story. It seems to me also important that such devices are signalled.

- *Sequence of events altered, condensed or left out*. Life is a messy business — many things happen at once, not all of them related to each other, and not necessarily unfolding at the same rate. You may want to write, for example, about the break-up with your husband, which happened at the same time as you started taking violin lessons and at the same time as your mother had a car accident and you were visiting her every day and at the same time as your son had a run-in with a teacher at school. What happens if you change the order of certain events, or put a number of events together and write them as one, for example, condensing five visits to your mother into one? Or leave out half the violin lessons? Or minimise the son's run-in with the teacher even though it was hugely distressing at the time?

It's important when faced with these kinds of decisions to examine why you are writing the memoir. Is it a legal record of the time? Probably not. Is it a history for the future? Maybe. Is it to convey selected strands of the pattern of life at a particular time? Probably. And then you need to examine your motives. Why are you leaving these events out? Is it because you would be embarrassed? Because you want to protect someone? Because you want to change the way the reader perceives what happened? There are any number of reasons to alter events in some way, but for me, the reason needs to be based on two criteria: first, does the alteration change the truth I want to convey? And second, does it affect the structure? If it clarifies the truth and if it creates a stronger, more effect-ive structure, then go ahead. If you cut and condense some of the visits to your mother or alter the sequence of violin lessons, it may convey the counterpointed difficulty of these two experiences more effectively and at the same time improve the structure by eliminating repetition.

- *Collapsed or left-out characters.* Scenes and events in life often have too many characters. Or too many for the writer to manage, at least. Perhaps I am speaking person-ally here — I come from a family of eight children so most events in my childhood involved a large cast! If

I write about my family, it can become too crowded on the page, too many names for the reader to keep track of. People, however, are much more problematic than events to 'collapse', that is, making two or more characters into one. You can almost hear them objecting as you try to melt them into someone else. Certainly, I don't feel justified in eliminating or condensing any of my brothers and sisters! The crowded confusion of family is part of the truth of my childhood experience.

But memoirists occasionally feel the need to collapse characters, especially peripheral ones, for reasons of economy and avoiding repetition — and sometimes to avoid identification. Television presenter, essayist and poet Clive James admits in the prologue of his *Unreliable Memoirs* to having put people he knew 'through the blender' so that they could not be recognised. In *Whatever The Gods Do*, I combined elements of two choir teachers, not because I didn't value their individuality, but because it would have been clumsy and repetitive to have both teachers at that point in the structure of the narrative. It is still truthful to the experience of being in the choir — I made nothing up — but in life, one teacher left to get married and another one arrived. It didn't seem necessary to my story to include this information.

I have also left people out of memoirs for a number of other reasons. In one memoir, a woman was omitted entirely because her presence represented another narrative strand which I decided was not mine to tell. It was also clear that 'structurally' her narrative, being emotionally powerful, would have overbalanced the feeling and shape of the narrative I was exploring. Elsewhere, I have left out people simply because to include them would have crowded the page with names.

Leaving people out is often a structural decision, but again, it can be to protect oneself or others. For example, you might decide to leave out an affair you had because you want to protect that person's present marriage — an important character is thus left out of your memoir. But a memoirist is not necessarily recording the whole truth of a particular time or experience; as the writer, she is deciding what elements of experience she wants to explore. If leaving out certain elements means leaving out people who were there at the time, then that is the memoirist's decision. Of course, it is important not to use this reasoning as an excuse to distort or misrepresent other people.

Keeping trust

Keeping the trust of your reader does not necessarily mean you do not ever invent anything, but I believe it does mean that you let the reader know in some way what is true and what is imagined. It does not apply to novels, of course, because the expectations we bring to our reading depend on the genre. When we read a novel, we expect that perhaps the writer has drawn on some of their own experience, but that the narrative and characters unfold according to the demands of the imagination. In a memoir, we expect that the narrative and characters unfold according to the demands that life has made. As in life, readers of memoir need to know what is true and what is invented if they are to give emotional and intellectual credence to your words. There are a few ways you can signal to your reader how to weigh what you have written.

- *The dedication or prologue statement.* Simply mention in the dedication or prologue that you have put characters through a blender or that you have used your imagination to convey a truth the facts could not supply or that you have invented scenes as a literary device.

- *The Mary McCarthy option.* In *Memories of a Catholic Girlhood*, McCarthy wrote her stories as she liked to remember them; then, tempering the desire to fictionalise for the sake of a good story with the need for honesty, she created inter-chapters that tell the reader what she has inferred or invented. This technique needs to be lightly used to avoid coming across as pedantic.

- *Layout design.* Using a layout device such as a different font or a narrower line can suggest that the section is to be read differently. Readers will soon work out whether it is a leap back in time, a different perspective, or an imagined sequence based on the facts. You can also use subtitles with a question mark to suggest that the section has been imagined.

- *Unreliable narrator option.* Suggest in the title or within the text that you, as narrator, might not be entirely reliable. You can suggest that your memory is faulty, that you have a propensity for exaggerating, that you don't have enough respect for the facts. Paradoxically, confessing your un-reliability makes you more trustworthy. At least we know to take what you say with a grain of salt.

- *Confess to imagining events.* Within the story, indicate that what you are about to write, or have written, is invented. In *The Last One Who Remembers*, after a piece on a child-hood cruelty, I wrote:

I could've gone to Confession. Except it didn't happen exactly the way I've told it. Although I conceived the evil, my brother carried it out. I, a voyeur, watched. And no-one threw the skull away; Denise's mother ran over it in her car. And I don't think we went so far in our lust for cruelty. Or is it only that I hope we didn't? The bowerbird is fabricating pieces from old magazine stories and school photographs and broken pieces of sacred paintings.

Such a device is direct and easy to use and clearly signals how the passage is to be read.

Where you stand on the border between fiction and memoir depends on your own sensibility as a writer and as a person. If you do not feel comfortable with any of these devices, if only the facts related in the right order at the right time feels truthful, then that is what you must do. As a memoirist myself, I do not mind altering the sequence or deleting a few elements, especially for structural demands, but each time it is crucial that I examine my motives and make sure I am not deceiving myself, let alone my readers. It is important that I try to tell the truth of my own perceptions as accurately as possible. Truth may be a construct, but truthfulness is not. It takes long and hard work to hit the pure metal of truthfulness — the ego is a constant and wily deceiver — but you always know when you have finally found some truthfulness in yourself. There is a clear unalloyed ring to it.

READING

The Last One Who Remembers

by Patti Miller

When I told my mother I wanted to write stories about the Great Aunts because I didn't want their lives to disappear, a 'look' came over her face.

'You know,' she said, 'Josie once said that when she died there would be no evidence of her having lived. She said that when she was gone and the last person who remembered her died, it would be as if she never existed.'

Do lives untold disappear without trace? Once the last
living memory of them is gone, what then? A life without
trace may easily be said to have not happened at all. Do we
all want to leave evidence, scratch 'I was here' on the
world like mindless tourists?

'But how can you write about them?' My mother
looked at me doubtfully. She was beginning to realise I
didn't have her respect for the facts. 'You barely remember
them. And Josie died before you were born, so did Mona
for that matter. And you were a little girl when Madge
died, and Allie.'

'What about Mona?' I asked.

'I never knew her. She died when she was eleven.'

'So there's no one left alive who knew her?'

'Well, I don't suppose so. She died in the early 1900s.
Imagine poor Grandma Reidy. Losing her husband and
then her baby and then little Mona, all within two years.
I don't know how she survived.'

I was more curious about Mona. She died near the end
of childhood. There is no physical trace of her life and no
direct memory of her in anyone's mind.

The impression her life has made on the world
seems fainter than a fingertip pressed on the ocean.
There is no sign that she giggled helplessly with her
sisters, swung her legs on the front porch, stole
cornflowers from the lady next door, drew a crayon
picture of the castle she would live in when she grew
up. She must enter the told world via a third-hand
memory if she is to exist past that brief moment in the
breathing world. Whatever the reason, I cannot bear for
Mona to have existed without trace. Surely, no one could
mind if I gave her breath and speech again. I have no
solid materials to work with, only the watered silk and

lace of invention. It flaps in the wind as it is placed in
the bower.

Mona's story?

The blue garden was the last thing to be left in one piece.
Mona spent a lot of time there because it was the only
place that hadn't come apart. She had made it herself, perhaps that was why it stayed together so long. Or perhaps it
was because of Baby. She knew Baby came to her garden.

It was down the yard behind the passionfruit trellis.
Nothing had been planted there because it was always in
the shade. The ground was cool and often damp, although
in the summer it would get dusty. It was about a yard wide
and three yards long, like a short path. Mona had paved it
with the broken blue platter and then put bricks either
end. She pressed the blue pieces in with little stones
between them, making a diagonal pattern. That was the
first thing she did …

… She was almost eleven when Baby died. He was only
one and a half years old. They had already left the hotel
and moved into this dark house. Mona thought everything
was going to come back together. Of course, she knew
Father wasn't coming back, and she knew they wouldn't
live in the hotel anymore. She couldn't feed the travellers'
horses in the stables out the back, or make butter with
Mother in the big kitchen. But they were here in
this house and she had a room with Allie and Ruby.
She put her glass ballerina and deer on the side of the
dressing-table.

Then Mother had grown fat and her skin glistened and
then Baby came. At first she was surprised when Baby
came. He was a boy, which was strange. There were no

boys in their family. Baby had blue eyes like Father and
sometimes, Mother laughed. They all lived in the little
dark house, except Madge, and Mona thought things
had stopped changing. Now they would stay the same,
unbroken. Mother was slim and straight again and
worked with Ruby in the garden when she had tidied
up the house.

Mother should have known Baby wouldn't last. She
shouldn't have loved him so much.

In *The Last One Who Remembers*, I explore the nature and
impact of stories in my life. It is clear in this extract that the
story of Mona is imagined. It was true that there were three
deaths in two years and I knew a few facts my mother had
told me about the family hotel, including the making of
butter. I had seen inside the house they moved to and some
of the crockery, although not a blue platter. The making of a
tiled garden with a broken plate was something I did myself
as a child. This fictional segment is part of the layering of
stories, real and imagined, which make up this memoir.

WRITING EXERCISES

1. Imaginary diary

Construct a diary of a three-month period in your life when
you did not keep a diary. Entries can be as frequent or as
irregular as you like, but remember, you can only know what
you know on that day, for example, if you are writing about a
custody battle, you can only write the pleasant telephone
conversation you had with your ex-spouse on a specific day,
uncoloured by the fact that you now know it was a ploy for a
kidnapping the next day. (A constructed diary is a useful

device, too, for putting events in sequence when there has been a jumble of overwhelming experiences.) *(1 hour)*

2. Journal entry

Construct one entry in a journal as if written by someone who is important in your life. Have them exploring an event or issue in relation to you. Remember it has to be from their perspective and in their voice. *(30 minutes)*

3. Remembering conversation

Write a scene, including some dialogue, which someone has told you about, but at which you were not present. It could even be a scene from before you were born — something your mother has recounted to you. *(30 minutes)*

4. Collapsing events

Select an event which occurred a number of times in the period you want to write about — it could be anything from going to the same holiday spot as a child, to visiting an aging parent in hospital over a few weeks or months. Collapse or combine the several events into one event — that is, as if the various experiences all happened in the same time sequence. *(30 minutes)*

13.

A REITERATION

WRITERS ARE ENDLESSLY hungry to learn more about writing. We think, talk, read, about writing because it's the most fascinating topic in the world. The endless dancing struggle to persuade words to convey our experience of being, or at least to construct a convincing parallel reality on the page, is enough to keep us occupied all day, every day. All the while, we know there is only one real way to keep developing as a writer, and that is to write. We nourish ourselves with the words of other writers to broaden and deepen our own experience of writing, and then we do it ourselves.

It seems to me that there are three essential things to keep in mind; all the rest can be used or kept aside as necessary.

1. Write your world with clear attention to the detail of being here. However dark or light your experience, clarity of observation will yield truth and beauty of style.

2. Write because it matters to you. However sardonic or passionate your attitude, your voice will have the beauty of truthfulness.
3. Write with the sense that you are making something. However correct or chaotic your experience, your writing will have beauty and truth of form.

Apparently Michelangelo left some advice for one of his drawing students scribbled on a piece of paper. It said, 'Draw, Antonio, draw, Antonio, draw and do not waste time.' Although I don't mind a little time-wasting every now and then — a quiet period of apparent inaction can help refresh the writing mind — it is still excellent advice: write, Antonio, write, Antonio, write and do not waste time. Now it is time to put this book down and start writing.

READING LIST

This is by no means a comprehensive or even a bare essentials reading list. It consists simply of the memoirs and other sources mentioned in *The Memoir Book*.

Memoirs and travel

Ashworth, Andrea, *Once in a House on Fire*, Picador, London, 1999.

Bauby, Jean-Dominique, *The Diving Bell and the Butterfly*, Fourth Estate, London, 1997.

Berendt, John, *Midnight in the Garden of Good and Evil*, Random House, New York, 1999.

Blixen, Karen, *Out of Africa*, Penguin, London, 1954.

Burroughs, Augusten, *Running with Scissors*, Hodder Headline, Sydney, 2003.

Burton, Richard, *The Pilgrimage to Al Medina and Mecca*, Dover, New York, 1964.

Byron, Robert, *The Road to Oxiana*, Penguin Books, London, 1992.

Capp, Fiona, *That Oceanic Feeling*, Allen & Unwin, Sydney, 2003.

Dalrymple, William, *The White Mughals*, Viking Penguin, India, 2002.

Davidson, Robyn, *Desert Places*, Penguin, New York, 1997.

De Blasi, Marlena, *A Thousand Days in Venice: An Unexpected Romance*, Allen & Unwin, Sydney, 2002.

De Botton, Alain, *The Art of Travel*, Hamish Hamilton Penguin, London, 2002.

Didion, Joan, *The Year of Magical Thinking*, Fourth Estate, London, 2005.

Dillard, Annie, *Pilgrim at Tinker Creek*, Harper & Row, New York, 1974.

Durrell, Gerald, *My Family and Other Animals*, Penguin, London, 2004.

Erdrich, Louise, *The Blue Jay's Dance*, HarperPerennial, New York, 1995.

Gray, Spalding, *Swimming to Cambodia*, Theatre Communications Group, New York, 1985.

Hakluyt, Richard, *Voyages to the New World*, Macmillan, London, 1972.

Hazzard, Shirley, *Greene on Capri*, Farrar, Straus and Giroux, New York, 2001.

Heyerdahl, Thor, *Kon-Tiki: Across the Pacific by Raft*, Rand McNally, New York, 1966.

Holdforth, Lucinda, *True Pleasures: A Memoir of Women in Paris*, Vintage, Sydney, 2004.

Inglis, Cecilia, *Cecilia: An Ex-Nun's Extraordinary Journey*, Penguin, Melbourne, 2003.

James, Clive, *Unreliable Memoirs*, Pan Macmillan, London, 1984.

Lewis, Elaine, *Left Bank Waltz*, Vintage, 2006.

McCarthy, Mary, *Memories of a Catholic Girlhood*, Harcourt Brace Jovanovich, New York, 1972.

McCourt, Frank, *Angela's Ashes*, HarperCollins, London, 1996.

Macdonald, Sarah, *Holy Cow*, Bantam, Sydney, 2002.

Miller, Patti, *The Last One Who Remembers*, Allen & Unwin, Sydney, 1997.

— *Whatever The Gods Do*, Vintage, Sydney, 2003.

Millet, Catherine, *The Sexual Life of Catherine M*, Serpent's Tail, London, 2002.

Modjeska, Drusilla, *Poppy*, McPhee Gribble, Melbourne, 1990.

Nabokov, Vladimir, *Speak Memory*, Vintage, New York, 1989.

Naher, Gaby, *The Truth About My Fathers*, Random House, Sydney, 2002.

Naipaul, VS, *India: A Wounded Civilisation*, Picador, London, 2002.

— *Beyond Belief*, Penguin, New Delhi, 1998.

O'Faolain, Nuala, *Are You Somebody?*, Hodder & Stoughton, London, 1997.

Phillips, Caryl, *The European Tribe*, Vintage, 2000.

Polo, Marco, *Travels of Marco Polo*, Jonathan Cape, London, 1928.

Rogers, Skye, *Drink Me*, Fourth Estate, Sydney, 2006.

Sayer, Mandy, *Velocity*, Random House, Sydney, 2005.

Slater, Nigel, *Toast*, Fourth Estate, London, 2003.

Stevenson, Robert Louis, *Travels with a Donkey in the Cevennes*, Chatto & Windus, London, 1987.

Stopes, Marie C, *A Journal from Japan*, Blackie, London, 1910.

Tristan, Flora, *Memoirs and Peregrinations of a Pariah*, Virago Beacon Travellers, London, 1987.

Turnbull, Sarah, *Almost French*, Bantam, Sydney, 2002.

Varga, Susan, *Heddy and Me*, Penguin, Sydney, 1994.

Varga, Susan and Coombs, Anne, *Broomtime*, Hodder Headline, Sydney, 2000.

Wearing, Deborah, *Forever Today*, Doubleday, London, 2005.

White, Edmund, *The Flâneur: A Stroll through the Paradoxes of Paris*, Bloomsbury, London, 2001.

Novels/short stories

Allende, Isabel, 'Tosca' in *The Stories of Eva Luna,* Penguin, London, 1991.

Haddawy, Husain (ed.), *1001 Arabian Nights*, Everyman's Library, London, 1992.

Miller, Henry, *Tropic of Cancer*, Jack Kahane, Paris, 1934.

Proust, Marcel, *In Search of Lost Time*, Penguin Classics, London, 2003.

Süskind, Patrick, *Perfume*, Penguin, London, 1986.

Writing books

Atkinson, Robert, *The Gift of Stories*, Bergin & Garvey, Westport, 1995.

Forster, EM, *Aspects of the Novel*, Pelican, London, 1985.

Miller, Patti, *Writing Your Life: A Journey of Discovery*, Allen & Unwin, Sydney, 2001.

Strunk, William and White EB, *The Elements of Style*, Macmillan, New York, 1979.

Zinsser, William (ed.), *Inventing the Truth: The Art and Craft of Memoir*, Houghton Mifflin Co, Boston, 1987.

Articles/essays

Aciman, Andre, 'Lies Sweet Lies', *Sydney Morning Herald*, 9 September 2000.

Baker, Russell, 'Life with Mother' in *Inventing the Truth: The Art and Craft of Memoir,* edited by William Zinsser, Houghton Miffin Co, Boston, 1987.

Campbell, Joseph, *The Hero with a Thousand Faces*, HarperCollins, New York, 1990.

Lopate, Phillip, *The Art of the Personal Essay*, Doubleday, New York, 1994.

Miller, Patti, 'Get the drift', S*ydney Morning Herald*, 23 November 2000.

Smith, Deborah, 'Once More With Feeling', *Sydney Morning Herald*, 2 April 2001.

Witze, Alexandra, 'Fragrant Memories', *Sydney Morning Herald*, 16 October 2004.

Woolf, Virgina, *Women and Writing*, Harcourt Brace Jovanovich, New York, 1980.

Poetry

Thomas, Dylan, *Under Milkwood*, JM Dent & Sons, London, 1975.

Keats, John, 'Ode On A Grecian Urn', in *The Poetical Works of John Keats*, Oxford Universiy Press, Oxford, 1922.

Unpublished manuscripts

Jobbins, Sheridan, 'Run Baby, Run'.

McGrory, Jenette, 'Train Crash'.

For writing workshops and manuscript assistance with memoir or autobiography: www.lifestories.com.au

ACKNOWLEDGEMENTS

THE AUTHOR AND publishers are grateful to the following for permission to reproduce copyright material:

New Island Books, Ireland, for extract from *Are You Somebody?* by Nuala O'Faolain © 1996

Harper Collins UK for extract from *The Diving Bell and the Butterfly* by Jean-Dominique Bauby © 1997

Theatre Communication Group for extract from *Swimming to Cambodia* by Spalding Gray © 1985

Skye Rogers for extract from *Drink Me* published by Fourth Estate, Australia © 2006

The Random House Group Ltd and The Curtis Brown Group Ltd, London, for extract from *Forever Today* by Deborah Wearing © 2005, published by Doubleday

Hodder Headline Hachette Livre and Atlantic Books Ltd for extract from *Running with Scissors* by Augusten Burroughs © 2002

HarperCollins UK for extract from *The Year of Magical Thinking* by Joan Didion © 2005

Random House Australia for extract from *True Pleasures: A Memoir of Women in Paris* by Lucinda Holdforth © 2003

Random House UK for extract from *In Search of Lost Time* by Marcel
Proust, translated by CK Scott Moncrieff.

Thank you also to Sheridan Jobbins for extracts from her manuscript, 'Run Baby, Run' and Jenette McGrory for extracts from her
manuscript, 'Train Crash'. Thank you, too, to all my memoir students,
from whom I have learned so much.

Finally, I would also like to thank Annette Barlow, Christa Munns
and Jo Jarrah, all of whom have looked after my words with such care.

INDEX